# THE CULTURE BLUEPRINT

Version 1.5

# FREE AUDIOBOOK!

You can give your whole company the book for free, and they can choose how they listen. Just remember, don't make it mandatory!

To get your free audio book, go to:
**www.CultureBlueprint.com/audiobook**

# PRAISE FOR
## *THE CULTURE BLUEPRINT*

"I am an avid reader, a really avid reader. No business book has ever brought me to such a highly emotional state that I have had tears welling up in my eyes. Your book has had that effect on me. Why? Because it creates practical and implementable methods and processes and hope that many people can have deeply meaningful and rewarding work. That includes CEO's, C level executives, and all the way through to the new hire, and on to it's customers and shareholders."

— **Gordon McDougall**, entrepreneur

"This book is one of the most interesting and comprehensive business guides I've ever read — and I've read quite a few. I can't even imagine starting a business today, without The Culture Blueprint by my side. Get your hands on it when it comes out! I personally guarantee you'll be glad you did."

— **Steve Dorfman**, host of *We Mean Business!*

"A lot of people who attended are still talking about you and asking how they can get in touch with you and your book. Great job! The experience was AWESOME and ACHIEVED!! Thanks so much for totally blowing my expectation clear out of the water!"

— **Beena Patel**, Toyota Financial Services, US Headquarters

"I was simply blown away. I read *The Culture Blueprint* and it transformed the way I think about my companies. I brought Robert in for a speech, and he did more than just talk about culture, he gave us an *experience* that became a catalyst moment. The teams not only saw the importance of a strong culture, they are now excited about it and realize it's everyone's responsibility, not just mine as CEO. Rather than viewing this as a mandatory program forced on them from outside, *they* are now excited about co-creating *and* maintaining strict adherence to these core values! I'm confident that if we ever veer off course, we have this shared experience to remember and reconnect us with what's really important. Any company could benefit from Robbe's wisdom. However, if you're a growing company, it's imperative that you speak with him immediately to harness the chaos, catalyze the vision, and stabilize for the future."

— **James Wallace**, CEO Scorpio Media

# FOREWORD

In 2003 I was the Associate Dean of the USC Marshall School of Business, and I had just written *The Coaching Revolution*. I met Robert Richman (we call him Robbe) at Georgetown University's coaching program and we've had a close professional relationship ever since.

Robbe has a unique perspective on the world, and it gives him unique insights. He was part of our team when we published *Tribal Leadership*, and without his effort, the book would never have hit the *New York Times* bestseller list. He challenged us to think like leaders, not just authors. As authors who wrote about leadership, we found this annoying! But trust me, having Robbe challenge you is one of the most important career and company-builders there is.

As we took his advice — grudgingly at first, then enthusiastically — and doors opened that we never imagined might crack. From arranging our first speech at Google to facilitating our meetings with the leadership at Zappos.com, he connected us to some of the most important people for us to meet. Robbe is a connector because he sees where things are things are going, and can nudge you to get there a little bit ahead of everyone else.

Robbe produced the audio book of *Tribal Leadership* and arranged for Zappos to sponsor the book, offering it digitally to all of their millions of customers. When they saw how well he could execute, Zappos quickly took Robbe away from us to launch Zappos Insights, the division that teaches company culture and customer service.

Zappos Insights was a brilliant idea, but ideas don't implement themselves. Again, it was something he had never done before, but his combination of ingenuity, drive, and leveraging his network of superstars (that I'm proud to be a part of) took this simple idea into what I would call the best corporate immersion experience in the world.

*The Culture Blueprint* is a portion of Robbe's brain in a book. It covers his time at Zappos Insights, and distills his thousands of conversations with business leaders of all types. He's turned that knowledge into 200 pages of actionable insights.

As is often true with new perspectives, some will strike you as original, and others as counterintuitive. My suggestion is to try them, and see what happens. Some will click, like a key made a lock, and others are still worth considering as they will lead you to your own insights.

In November, 2012, I had finished day two of a three-day event called "Leadership Unleashed," when my taxi was hit by another car. I woke up hours later in the UCLA medical center with a shattered jaw, a severe concussion, and lucky to be alive. The next morning, with only an hour preparation, Robbe filled in for me with a speech that had everyone buzzing. You want him in your bullpen, and I'm thankful he's in mine.

**Dave Logan**
Co-Author of *Tribal Leadership*

# FOREWORD TO THE 1.5 UPDATE

I was standing in the center of Zappos Insights, talking directly to the manager, Rob Richman. Without even knowing me, he gave me one of the highest compliments. He said, "I've seen thousands of people come through the Zappos tour and you have the best questions I've ever heard."

As Rob will tell you, when it comes to culture, the most valuable leaders don't claim to have all the answers. They can't! A culture is not completely shaped by any one person. The most valuable leaders tend to have the best questions — because questions tend to create engaging conversations, and can lead us to think for ourselves. The best leaders don't routinely tell people what to do. They create a set of conditions where leadership can emerge.

Since that fateful day at Zappos, we've been good friends…and I've had a front row seat watching Rob himself emerge as a leader.

Professionally, I am a management consultant. I coach software teams and their organizations achieve higher levels of measurable performance by using "agile" principles and practices. And so eventually, Rob brought me in to teach his team how to be agile, and boy did they succeed. As Rob lead that team, "Zappos Insights" went from a concept in the CEO's head to a multi-million dollar Zappos subsidiary company with 25,000 customers a year.

When I launched the annual CultureCon conference (an event focused on company culture), I naturally invited Rob to participate as our keynote speaker. His keynote speech set the pace, tone and tempo for the entire event.

I help the best companies in the world to implement agile in pursuit of stronger results. And I routinely invite Rob to help me to do work inside world-class organizations like INTUIT. I bring Rob to plan and facilitate high-impact, enterprise-wide "Open Space" meetings. These are extremely important events in my work with clients and Rob always delivers the goods.

Rob is like a utility player for innovative companies, delivering speeches, workshops, meetings, coaching. He can walk into any culture, any organization, without prior knowledge, observe, and diagnose what's really going on.

I'm honored to be a part of this book, not only via this foreword, but also as the guest author of the chapter on creating highly engaging meetings. It is indicative of our constant collaboration on thought leadership in the field of culture. Rob is one of my "thinking partners." Interacting with Rob always helps to clarify my thinking about key ideas around culture and culture design.

Businesses that acknowledge the intentional design and maintenance of a well-formed company culture create a huge and lasting competitive advantage. The book you hold in your hands is a culture design manual...designed to be useful for analyzing, designing, testing, debugging, installing and maintaining a company culture that can bring *higher performance* to your business.

Robert's passion for culture and culture dynamics come shining through in this handbook. It's my hope you will study this book very carefully, as you consider how you might use culture design principles to encourage greatness — and great *results* — in your own organization.

**Daniel Mezick**, author of *The Culture Game*
www.DanielMezick.com
North Guilford, Connecticut, USA
Monday, September 8, 2014

# TABLE OF CONTENTS

# VERSION 1.5
## (UPGRADES AND BUG FIXES)

It was a year since I had published The Culture Blueprint 1.0 to a limited "beta" audience. I thought of the book like software. It needed to be tested first. The responses astounded me. The first reader said he was literally in tears with the possibility this created for a business. Others would ask if they could buy copies for their staff, or interview me for their blogs. And yet...I considered the book a failure.

No matter how many positive comments came in, only one thing mattered to me — actual results. And I wasn't hearing enough. I heard a lot of stories of hope, passion, enthusiasm and drive, but I didn't hear enough success stories for me to take it out of beta.

I decided to focus on my consulting — rolling up my sleeves and doing the work. Companies would hire me to do a culture due diligence, and I would spend several days talking and observing, then compiling a report to show what was really going on. I would end it with clear action steps. And then...I would rarely hear anything back. Leaders found my report useful and insightful, but where were the sweeping changes, the transformation of culture?

I was so frustrated with both my book and my consulting that I almost gave up on both of them. That's when I realized, ironically, *that giving up is exactly what it would take to make it work.*

I got a call from a conservative business owner who had heard my speech, read my book and wanted to bring me in to help them figure out their vision and their values — all within one day. I told him it wasn't impossible. The process I outlined would take at least 6 months, and even if we *could* do it in a day, there was no way we could get his team of eight highly contentious and passionate businessmen to agree.

But he was determined, and his desire inspired me to throw out my playbook and start fresh. I took an approach that allowed the team to guide their business culture, instead of me. To my great surprise, by using principles of self-organization rather than focusing on me as the guru, they had their vision and values by the end of the day.

From that point, I decided to change up my business model. I no longer wanted to be the guru of culture. In fact, to be successful, I knew I had to essentially disappear. I wanted the leaders and the teams to get the credit for designing their own culture, because if they could do it for themselves, then it would last.

Now when I facilitate they don't talk about me afterward, they talk about how much they love the process and how empowered they feel as leaders. I successfully disappeared and let the culture take center stage.

I then realized that *The Culture Blueprint 1.0* was not a failure. In fact it's a strong operating system for any company. What was missing until now was the *installer program* for this software. Thanks to these experiences as well as my partnership with the master of emerging culture, Daniel Mezick (author of *The Culture Game*), I realized that a business owner cannot mandate a change within their company. It must be done collaboratively with the team. And I will show you how.

The biggest update to version 1.5 is the chapter "The Installer." If you only read this one chapter, it will upgrade any change you are planning at your company. The *Culture Blueprint 1.0* was a solid piece of software for the organization, but the installer was buggy. I'm proud to say it's been fixed, and it is safe to use, enterprise-wide.

# ACKNOWLEDGMENTS

First, I have to thank Tony Hsieh, CEO of Zappos, for betting on me. Before he hired me, I had no experience in corporate culture, or launching a product offering like Zappos Insights, but he and Aaron Magness saw my passion and determination. My world has never been the same.

The Zappos Insights team helped to create the learning environment where I obtained many of the insights for this book. We had an epic time together launching a start-up within Zappos. Thanks Missy, Marie, Andi, Jenna, Corey, Mig, Rocco, Renae, Valerie, Natalie, Danni, Elia, Pam, Trish, Jon, Squeezy, Crystal and Mike. A big thank-you to goals coach Augusta Scott, who has created breakthroughs for so many people. And a huge thank-you to my original partner in crime, Donavon Roberson. I couldn't have done any of this without you, man.

Another big thank-you goes to another Insights team member, who has been with me through many ventures: Beth Kirlin. Thank you for constantly backing me up and being a partner in so many ways through life. Dad, thank you for your constant encouragement to me as a writer (and as a mentor in business). Bill, thank you for paving the way.

Thank you to Dave Logan, who has opened up so many doors and has been a great friend and mentor. Thanks also to Daniel Mezick, a true master of culture who has influenced so much of my thinking and to Michael Margolis for all your support and keeping me from taking things too seriously. Joey Coleman, thank you for loading on the pressure through the years. Charles Planck, you're always inspiration through everything, no matter what I do.

I never would have started without Chance Barnett's "writing hack." He said, "The one trick I'm going to give you is the one you don't want to hear: Just write it." Thank you, Chance. And thank you for the information product inspiration, Eben Pagan, Mike Koenigs and Pam Hendricksen.

Finally, a big thank-you for all the great feedback on this book goes to Michael Liskin, Todd Staples, Cliff Michaels, Kathleen O'Malley, and Carrie Kish. (Your ass-kicking is priceless.)

# INTRODUCTION

All business innovation seems counter-intuitive before it becomes common sense. Just imagine yourself running a factory at the turn of the twentieth century. Your workers are cranking out widgets, and you're happy to have them for twelve hours a day at a minimal cost. You're proud of your efficiency, and you feel good knowing that you're giving jobs to people who would otherwise be in poverty.

Then one day you hear about a factory that is giving its people paid time off (vacations and breaks). The idea sounds shocking: "What? How can you pay people NOT to work? You're losing efficiency!" And of course you would be right — in the short term. However, in the long term, that brave factory would experience fewer injuries, lower turnover, and greater morale than any other company. Today this policy is so common that it's no longer just a best practice, it's the law.

We are now at a similar turning point. We are going through a big shift in business away from a system that was focused completely on metrics and into one where performance is driven by focusing on the people who deliver it. A purely metrics-focused business is the equivalent of a sports team watching the scoreboard throughout the game. But as we all know, it's actions and behaviors that drive points, baskets, touchdowns, and runs — not a focus on the score.

Companies like Zappos, Google, and Apple have shifted from metrics as the key focus (while still tracking them intensely) to values. Note that each of these companies has quite different *values*. Zappos is based on service and happiness. Apple is based on design and excellence. Google is based on academics and engineering. Each culture is different, and yet each company operates from the same key principles.

If you've read about these companies, you may have heard about their approaches and their techniques. You may have tried to duplicate these, but the truth is that every business is unique, and it's their home-grown culture that drives their success (not the other way around).

Most work on corporate culture has been in the form of academic exploration, case studies, and analysis of various tools and techniques. In contrast, *The Culture Blueprint* is actually a systematic guide to designing and transforming a culture.

For many years I have coached business leaders from various industries on how to improve their company cultures. I have been fortunate to work alongside world-changing companies like Google, Toyota, GM, and Eli Lilly, offering presentations and consulting. During these experiences, I have seen certain patterns emerge, I have learned what works and what doesn't, and I have accurately identified the leverage points where the magic of a culture shift can happen.

Ultimately, culture is about *people*, and people cannot be controlled. That said, like an architect of a house, you have an opportunity to design the structure that will create an experience for the people that live inside. And that experience will shape the behaviors and values that ultimately drive the actions that get you results.

You are about to discover the blueprint that will enable you to design this experience.

Since version 1.0 of this book, I've been asked, "Why a blueprint? Why architecture? You can't really design a culture because the people are in control." That is absolutely true, the same way the architect of a house cannot plan a happy family. The design comes in creating the optimal setting, flow and support to allow people to thrive.

Other changes to the updated version include tightened language, and a new team building section that integrates the previous "extra credit." Also included are a page on the types of values you can use, as well as a section on why agreement is the lynchpin of culture.

# WHO IS THIS BOOK FOR?

This book has several different possible audiences, all of whom can use it as a key in their everyday work:

- Executives looking to create a full-scale culture shift
- Managers who want to efficiently deliver results, while having a great time
- Anyone in an organization who cares about people, and wants to create a great place to work
- Consultants and coaches who advise companies on management and leadership
- Start-up founders who realize that culture drives revenue, productivity, and happiness, and want to get it right from the start
- Educators, teachers and theorists who want to learn what's really going on underneath the surface in most organizations
- Venture capitalists and advisory board members who want to give their investment companies an extra edge over their competition

If you fit one of the above categories, I believe you will gain great benefit from the years of knowledge and research that I have distilled in this book.

The strategies, processes, and techniques I describe I gathered primarily by studying the success of Zappos and using its culture as a model. (Zappos was rated #1 in Customer Service by American Express customers in 2011, and #6 Best Place to Work by Fortune Magazine in 2011.) I also have met with hundreds of the world's best companies, including Google, Eli Lilly, Intuit, Coca Cola, and Patagonia.

# PROBLEMS THIS BOOK WILL SOLVE

Almost all problems in an organization come back to culture issues. This book will teach you how to:

- ✔ Scale a great workplace as the company grows (with systems)
- ✔ Keep workers engaged (Create world-changing teams you don't have to motivate.)
- ✔ Keep morale high (You won't even need the word "morale" after this.)
- ✔ Get work done while having a great time (Work will become play.)
- ✔ Make innovation cheap and easy for everyone (You'll learn the key to innovation no one is talking about.)
- ✔ Create a place where everyone feels ownership of the company (so you can relax and focus on the future)
- ✔ Keep behavior professional without long manuals and policies (You'll learn the 99% rule.)
- ✔ Keep turnover extremely low (so competition will not be able to steal your talent)
- ✔ Utilize all the hidden talent in the organization (There is more energy in your organization than you know.)
- ✔ Keep customer service top of mind for employees at all levels (Customer service is the new edge, and you'll see why.)

You might think your culture is screwed up. You might be right, but we're not going to focus on that. Asking "Why?" almost always ends up being about a search for a single answer. But there is no single answer. A less-than-optimal business culture is always the result of many factors that operate together as a system, and they're usually invisible.

I have seen these techniques work regardless of a company's size, industry, demographics, or past history. In the words of Buckminster Fuller, "Things never change things by fighting the existing reality. To change something, build a new model that makes the existing model obsolete." And as you build this new model, whatever you need to know from the past will emerge.

### The two kinds of culture conversations: Which are you in?

In my thousands of conversations about culture, I realized all of them fit in either one of two categories. The first is a *conversation of limitations*. I hear all about the reasons something cannot change, or why the CEO will block it, or why the ship is hard to move. These are all valid points, and I actually think it's a good idea to get them all out onto the table. Go ahead and rant!

And when you're done, you're ready for the second type of conversation: *the conversation of possibilities*. This is when you go into a "What if…" state of mind. It's when you're open to new options; when you take a beginner's mindset and start to play with all the resources you have (because, once you list them, you will see you have a great wealth of assets).

### Culture change — in compressed time

*The Culture Blueprint* is a step-by-step process that will save you ten years of time. Here you will benefit from decades' worth of lessons learned from the best companies in the world. You won't have to guess or start from scratch.

### The best change of all

You won't actually see it until you take action, but the best part of this is that your home and personal life will completely change as a result of these practices. This is what Chris Widner, Director of Customer Service for Dyn, said after leaving the Zappos Insights Culture Boot Camp and making changes at his organization:

*"The positive changes didn't stay at the office alone. My wife immediately noticed the change in me. Instead of coming home exhausted and needing some 'me time,' I'm energized from the successes of the day and energized to see my family."*

# THE INSTALLER

*The Culture Blueprint* is an operating system to run your culture. However, if the installation process of this software is not done well, then it doesn't matter how robust it is. This section is all about how to carefully consider that installation.

Two of the core principles you'll read about in the book are:

**1. Co-create** – You can never shape culture alone.
**2. Opt-in** – Anything mandatory or forced will be met with resistance, whereas anything with invitation attracts the right people.

These principles are so fundamental and valuable that if you just get these two concepts, you could put down the rest of the book. I recommend reading this section again after you've read the rest of the book.

I first realized how vital these were when I was at a company that was about to roll out a process based on *The Lean Startup*, a popular book in the entrepreneurial community. The people really wanted it, and yet I noticed they were resisting it. The reason was because the way they did it was by a) forcing everyone to read the book and b) telling them how it would be rolled out.

This generated a lot of resentment. First, you can't make anyone read a book. The worst you could do is fire them for not reading it, and will you really let it come to that? Second, no one knows the business better than those actually doing the work. So when leadership mandated the process for carrying out an organizational change, they gave no credit to the experience and insight of the people. The result was resentment and resistance.

All of this could have been avoided through the very principles and actions outlined in this book, which will guide you through any organizational change you're looking to make.

### 1. Start with the real issue.

Forcing staff to read a book is really forcing a solution without first discussing the problem or the desired change. What is the real challenge? What do you want to solve? If you discuss this openly (inviting those who would like to discuss it), then you may get valuable information. This discussion is not meant to result in a solution; rather it should result in *fantastic questions.*

Einstein said if he had an hour to figure out a problem, he would spend most of the time defining the problem. A clearly defined problem paves the way for an elegant solution.

### 2. Discuss the book in the context of the problem.

Now that you've defined the problem, you can ask this group, "Does it make sense for all of us to read *The Culture Blueprint?*" Of course, I'm biased so I believe it will be quite helpful for any culture vision you have. That said, I am much more dedicated to your relationship to your team and your company than I am to selling more books. If your team is empowered to choose for themselves, then you've already made a big step in creating a strong culture.

### 3. Allow for self-organization.

As you'll read, there are many options in *The Culture Blueprint* — so many that you may be overwhelmed. This is where your team or co-workers can help. What idea resonates the most? Who has the passion for what? What would be safe to try? What has the highest leverage and is the best investment of your time and resources.

You'll find that you don't have to carry the burden of answering these questions alone. In fact, if you do, you'll likely get it wrong. Your team and your company are not only there to help, but, if they care, then they have a strong desire to help. You'll be increasing engagement by having them help with the decision.

In groups larger than a team, I highly recommend Open Space Technology. (See www.cultureblueprint.com/resources.) It's an open meeting format that will help you get the best ideas from the most passionate and inspired people. Rather than having leadership set the agenda, the entire group determines what they are passionate about and how to take responsibility for that.

# HOW THIS BOOK GOT STARTED

It was the summer of 2008. Had I been paying attention to the economy, I would have seen that a recession was coming, but my eyes were on a dotcom CEO who was more generous than any I had ever known. Tony Hsieh, the CEO of Zappos.com, was known for tweeting his location to employees, inviting them out for drinks, and meeting up with customers whenever he travelled.

Their headquarters in Henderson, Nevada, near Las Vegas, was becoming known as a virtual Disneyland of corporate happiness. More than any other company in the world, Zappos was famous for putting its employees first — a trend that I knew would explode. Meanwhile, customers would rave and blog and tweet about their outstanding level of customer service.

I sent Tony a copy of *Tribal Leadership*, a breakthrough book on culture I was marketing for the authors, Dave Logan, John King, and Halee Fischer Wright. Tony loved it and tweeted to the world that the book codified much of what Zappos had been doing instinctively.

The authors and I then went to Las Vegas to visit with the Zappos executive team to teach the deeper layers of Tribal Leadership. Afterward, Tony invited us to the merchandising group's happy hour that night, but before we went, he said, "We have a half hour to kill. You're welcome to wander the halls and talk to anyone you'd like."

That offer alone blew me away. Tony knew we were journalists and anything his staff of a thousand might say would go on the record. But that was the point. He regarded each employee as a culture ambassador for the brand. Most companies will only let the press converse with trained representatives who are limited to talking points. But Zappos didn't even have a PR department. It was remarkable.

Later, the "happy hour" we attended could hardly be called typical. When you use that expression in corporate America, it usually means forced awkwardness with co-workers after work. But instead of taking time away from people's families, Zappos starts its happy hours early, at 4:30. And it was more like a party than a simple cocktail hour. Drinks flowed, video skits played on a big screen, and karaoke soon followed. The bar was packed and you could tell that everyone wanted to be there. It was a total blast.

While the happy hour was ridiculously fun, I knew from my earlier conversation with the "ambassadors" that Zappos was not just all fun and games — it was really more like family. And you could feel it both inside and outside the office.

Then I came across an entry in their 2008 culture book. This is a compendium of unedited submissions from employees, along with photos from the year. (You can get one at www.CultureBook. org.) Story after story showed me how the company was changing employees lives for the better.

After my experience at Zappos, I knew I wanted to be a part of their culture in one way or another, and I realized how I could contribute to the larger story when Tony mentioned his idea for Zappos Insights.

Zappos was already being bombarded with requests for tours, meetings, and information about the company's processes. Everyone wanted to learn how they created such great customer service while making their employees happy. Tony saw a business idea in meeting these constant outside requests.

The only problem was that the company had no idea how to launch this type of business. They knew e-commerce. They knew how to create a direct-to-consumer brand. But this business would be a business-to-business information product, and they had no experience in the field.

Fortunately, I had been fascinated with this type of business. The margins are very high, and if the content is good, it can have a big impact and spread fast.

Zappos had previously tried to launch a video site with monthly subscriptions, but it flat-lined. After I shared my advice on new product launches and membership websites, Tony asked me if I would help them launch the new business idea. Together with Donavon Roberson, I was tasked with launching Zappos Insights with one strict caveat: no use of Zappos resources. That meant no web developers, no marketing resources — nothing from the consumer brand. The idea was to launch this as a "skunkworks" project, somewhat below the radar so that it had no chance of disturbing their consumer goods business.

So there we were, essentially about to launch a brand-new division of Zappos that first and foremost had to incorporate an amazing culture. It had the potential for success, but with limited resources and support, one key question remained:

*How do we even get started?*

We knew that people were the key component of the Zappos culture, so we decided to start by hosting a two-day event. Of course, this could not just be a bunch of PowerPoint slides in a hotel room. This had to be a Zappos experience.

So instead we brought our clients into the Zappos family by taking them through the office, putting them on the phones with call reps, allowing them to ask questions of our managers, and taking them out to dinner and drinks. We even took them to Tony's house to hang out and have fun.

We called it a "culture bootcamp," offering the managers and business leaders who came to us for help a living laboratory where they could experience and experiment with culture, in real time.

Our hope was that everyone would love the content, which we could then put online. This was our entire plan. How else would we get new members? We were surprised when the feedback showed that while the content was simply good, the experience was "mind-blowing." They said they did not fully believe how much change was possible until they got there. From that day forward the plan changed. We would not start Zappos Insights as a content company; we would start it as an *experience company*. It didn't take too long after that to realize that we were doing more than just creating experiences.

*We were a belief-changing company that happened to sell corporate training.*

But wait, what beliefs were we changing? We were sharing our idea that change was possible and that whatever you want to create in your business, you can create. You just have to believe it will work. People who did not believe it would come to Zappos Insights and experience it for themselves.

Here is feedback from one man's experience:

*"I just wanted to say that I TRULY believe that Zappos is changing the world. I envision that in 5, 10, 15, 20 years' time, many companies will have adopted an open, honest, friendly, and work-hard, play-hard culture in their workplace — following Zappos' lead."*

**— Rob Johnson**

While we had a hit on our hands, it still wasn't easy. We built out a whole suite of events and tours and rebuilt the membership site.

With our customers visiting us every day, we never had to leave the office to learn their challenges and frustrations. Being at Zappos Insights was like a customer lab where we could study our market in real time.

At first this was quite scary. Who were we to tell these Fortune 500 companies what to do? But we found that offering our stories, our questions, and our reflections helped them solve their own problems. And when they pioneered their own solutions, we could then share those stories with new customers. As our guests grew in number, so did our team, which begged the next question:

*How do we start to develop our team?*

Perhaps the greatest challenge was developing the team to execute our idea. We were turning a simple business idea into a multi-million dollar company, and that meant we had to grow fast. As a company within Zappos, we hired almost entirely from within. And no one (including me) had ever done what we were doing before. But we kept hiring people who loved core value #6: "Pursue growth and learning." We turned customer service agents into speakers, writers, planners, photographers, and video editors. Our operations person was a twenty-one-year-old woman who could grasp systems faster than anyone.

This is how I learned the "power" of empowerment.

Those were work hard, play hard days. Meeting the demand for events had us working constantly, figuring it out as we went (some would say making it up as we went). But we would also have fun. We would produce videos for our customers and then have a ball creating "blooper reels." And we would joke around a lot as we grew. (I was scared to leave sometimes because I would often come back to see my desk pranked.)

We had plenty of conflicts and differences of opinion to deal with, and it was a real challenge to keep the team happy while maintaining our double-digit growth rate. As we developed the team, we began to realize how our differences drove creativity and innovation, but we also had to learn how to deal with conflict and a variety of communication styles. It was like leadership boot camp.

**Having this direct experience with a growing, changing, and challenging culture full of diverse ideas and opinions was my best education. This is what I have to offer you in this book.**

As I began to travel, speak, and consult with more companies, I found patterns in both the problems and the solutions they faced. And as I started to repeat myself, I knew I had to get this information out in a way that could help people I didn't have the ability to visit.

Culture is such a big topic that people don't know where to start. They want a guide, a step-by-step plan, a blueprint. What you're now holding in your hands is a result of that need.

*The Culture Blueprint* is the compilation of all I learned as a result of:

- studying the Zappos culture for three years and learning how to share their mystique with the world;
- teaching, coaching, and consulting for hundreds of companies facing the challenges of growth and culture change; and
- building a company within Zappos and directly learning through all those challenges (sometimes very painfully).

It is an honor and a privilege to share this with you now.

You are more a part of the process than you know. I am independently publishing this version because my primary purpose is not to launch a bestseller. Rather, I want to provide information that works and gets you results. Then I want to hear from you about what worked. I will include your story in later versions to both acknowledge you and to help future readers. You can reach me at Robert@CultureBlueprint.com.

# HOW TO USE THIS BOOK

*The Culture Blueprint* enables you to start with a simple, vague notion of what you want, and end with a culture system running so well that you could package it and leave the company (if you wanted to, but why leave after you've designed your own world?).

Since the book represents an entire system, you'll want to read all the way through it. That said, you can get value at any point.

How you use this book will depend on the level of engagement that you're looking for at this time. Keep in mind that there are many ways you can experience a breakthrough with this book:

- It might be one small shift that does it for you. (Check out the "Immediate Wins" section.)
- You may be looking for a specific process or technique. (See the "Culture Toolkit" section.)
- You may want to align people to your vision. (See the "Vision" section.)
- You may want to eliminate toxic parts of your culture. (See the "Troubleshooting" section.)
- You might want a whole shift in mindset. (See the "Principles of Culture" section.)
- Maybe this information is not directly for your use, but you teach these principles to someone else.

Whether you want a full-scale culture shift, or you're starting from scratch, I recommend reading the whole book. Then, after reading it once, you might just pick it up every now and then as a reference.

# GET READY!

Before we do, let's get one thing clear here. Culture change is *not* a strategy or an initiative. This is a total mind shift. Once you truly experience it, you can't go back. It's like the Matrix.

And…Expect challenges, because that's what's life is. It's all about how we react to the challenges. Do you ever hear of soccer players whining that it's so annoying that there is a goalkeeper blocking their kicks? No! While there are clear rules, it's the obstacles that create the space for art.

We are going to spend a lot of time on the psychology, tools, and foundations of culture. This may frustrate some, and if so, you can skip all of this and go straight to the implementation sections. However, if you really want to "get" culture at a deep level, please dive in and drink it all up! It's like mastering anything.

For example, in sports, Hall of Fame athletes do not have a particular trick or technique that created their greatness. If they did, it could easily be copied. Instead, it's their mindsets and habits, and especially their practice time, that really drive their greatness. The majority of their time is spent preparing, off the field. A football game takes several hours to play, but the ball is only in motion for twelve minutes in an average game. Any ideas, plans or plays may suddenly change when everything becomes active. In business, you have to constantly "call an audible" (when a football quarterback notices the defensive lineup and changes the play by loudly voicing a new play change).

It's mindset and habits that drive behavior. If you know how these work, you will be able to analyze any culture immediately. Without this knowledge you will have to do everything by trial and error. Let's get into the principles so that you can skip years of experimentation.

# Chapter One

## Culture Architecture 101

## ⭕ WHAT IS CULTURE?

Think about how you would define "culture." What words come to mind? If you ask a room full of business people what culture is, you'll get many answers, such as:

*"It's people's attitudes."*
*"It's a set of beliefs."*
*"It's the way we do things around here."*
*"It's how we interact."*
*"It's what people really think of the organization."*
*"It's a set of habits."*

And you know what? They're all right, but they're all answering a different question. They are answering the question *"How do you notice culture?"* What they mention are all artifacts or evidence of culture. They all reveal the culture, but don't confuse the pointing finger with what it is showing.

Consider this: Culture can be experienced regardless of someone knowing the artifacts. And how is that? How can anyone simply walk into an organization and, within just a few interactions, "know" the culture without being able to articulate why?

Before we define culture for the purpose of the blueprint, let's take a look at how Wikipedia defines it:

**Culture** (from Latin *cultura;* literally "cultivation") is a term that has many different interrelated meanings. However, the word "culture" is most commonly used in three basic senses:

- Excellence of taste in fine arts and humanities, also known as high culture
- An integrated pattern of human knowledge, belief, and behavior that depends upon the capacity for symbolic thought and social learning
- The set of shared attitudes, values, goals, and practices that characterizes an institution, organization, or group

Once you have read the entire book, I recommend coming back to this page and re-reading these definitions. They are far more applicable than you can imagine.

Culture itself can be seen as a process starting from the basic human desire to create, which is expressed by the symbols or language we use to communicate, and finally by the tools that actively and consciously reflect it. Culture (like in a biology lab culture) is simply an environment to grow something. For the purpose of moving forward, let's create a very simple definition that will keep us focused on why we are discussing this in the first place.

## ○ THE SIMPLE IDEA BEHIND CULTURE

Try on this definition:

*Culture is a feeling.*

That's all it is. When you strip away all the language, interactions, and signs, you are simply left with a *feeling*, one that's created by the people you are with. Yes, it takes conversation to articulate it, but what you're left with is a feeling.

The easiest way to get in touch with that feeling is to have a stranger come into an organization's culture and interact for a day, asking questions and observing. That person will be able to describe to you the feeling they have upon exiting.

I learned this by speaking to a producer for the Harvard Business Review video publication. At the end of his three days, he sat me down and said, "I have visited the best companies in the world, and I've met with many heads of state. And I can tell you, I have never felt more embraced and welcomed than I have here at Zappos." With a tear in his eye, he added, "I want to bring my family back next time so that they can experience this."

So if culture is a feeling, what is it that creates feelings? Simply put, it is *experiences that create emotions*. Think of every single piece of information you learned in college. How much can you remember? Now think of your experiences in college — the events, parties, late-night conversations, sports games, and so on. Notice that it is the experience of something that lasts. All information, strategy, logistics — it's all forgotten.

*Experience makes the impact, not information.*

So as you read this book, together we are creating an experience right now. I have done my best to weave together words, models, structures, and examples so that you have a powerful experience that you can use as a reference point in developing your culture. What you may find surprising is that you may not remember most (or any) of the information. True learning and growth will happen as the result of taking the information and putting it into practice. You will gain priceless wisdom through *your own experience.*

But we're getting ahead of ourselves. You have a key decision to make right now, at this very moment: How will you use this reading to create an optimal experience for yourself? Will you do what most people do?

Most people:

 let a book lie on their desk, like a paperweight;

only pick up a book when they have a few spare moments;

read a couple of chapters, then stop when the content starts to challenge them;

read while constantly checking email and texting; or

read without a pen or a notebook to take down key points to remember.

Effective readers and action-oriented leaders:

 cut out all interruptions by phone and email so that they can focus;

set a calendar date to create the time and space;

write their key questions in the front of the book to focus their mind on getting the most value;

keep a notebook handy so they can centralize their ideas as they read;

write out their own index in the back of the book, based on key ideas, that they can easily reference later;

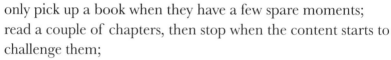

pick a key area of improvement that they will apply this to and plan that project as they go; and

 commit to teaching it to another person after reading it, so that they understand it at a deeper level.

Again, it's up to you to co-create this optimal experience with *The Culture Blueprint.* Pick one or two for your focus.

# ⭕ OLD MODEL VS. NEW MODEL OF MANAGEMENT CULTURE

Because most of modern business consists of communication, we can see the models of culture within language itself. Language shows how we got to where we are today.

The old model of business is based on command and control hierarchies. To see the old model in business, all we have to do is take a look at the language. As you take a look at the chart below, also notice where we derive our terms from, plus the evolutionary pattern.

| Military | Sports |
|----------|--------|
| Strategy | Coach |
| Recruit | Team |
| Train | Player |
| Fire | Partner |
| Execute | |
| Target | |
| Market | |
| Engage | |
| Employ | |
| Deploy | |

The predominant language of management is military-based, and war analogies have created a feeling of fear within organizations. This is because in war, land and natural resources are valued above any single life. But that's changing. People are becoming more and more important. So in the new model, relationships matter most because the previous needs have become cheap and commoditized. Now the edge comes in people, relationships, innovation, and information. All are connected.

In fact, I would venture to say that even though I do not know you personally, we actually do the same tasks every day. Do you read and write emails? Do you call people? Do you search for information on Google? Do you develop presentations, and plan out projects?

As I mentioned, almost all of business today has become communications. Therefore, we need a new way of speaking that is based on communications metaphors.

The most relevant metaphors involve communications: languages, codes, information, sender/receiver, transmissions, etc. Another set of related metaphors uses computer networks:

## Computer-based terms

| | |
|---|---|
| Network | Affiliate |
| Programming | Hub |
| Code | Beta |
| Architect | Hack |
| Design | Install |
| Host | Download |

The old management language actually mirrors the older computer language — Do you remember mainframes and dumb terminals? All commands would come from a centralized unit. Traditional hierarchies reflect that, and they can't adapt quickly enough to keep up with the rate of change. But now, we need a true peer-to-peer network to respond to today's business challenges.

Here are a few examples of where we are already seeing this play out:

**Network** – As Facebook (an international community four times as big as the population of the United States) has demonstrated, a "social network" has become one of the world's most valuable companies.

**Code** – Coders or programmers have become one of the most sought-after hires globally. This is because everything in our world is becoming an interface, a site, or an app. Media theorists such as Douglas Rushkoff have stated that those who don't understand programming will be left behind because our entire world is now based on code.

**Design** – Apple, the world's most valuable company, has shown that design can trump all other factors. In the words of Steve Jobs: "People think it's this veneer — that the designers are handed this box and told, 'Make it look good!' That's not what we think design is. It's not just what it looks like and feels like. Design is how it works." As culture designers, we are creating architecture to provide the best possible environment for people to thrive.

**Hack** – There is an emerging group of authors called "life hackers," such as Tim Ferriss, author of *The 4-Hour Workweek*. These are people who have figured out how something in life works (for example, sleep) and how to use minimal effort to change it for maximum gain. Hacking goes beyond programming when people realize that, like a computer network, all of life is made up of complex systems. And if we know the vulnerable points where a small action can have a big impact, then we can "hack" those systems.

Knowing how culture works as a system is one of the seven key principles of culture, which you are about to learn.

# ⭕ THE SEVEN PRINCIPLES OF CULTURE

### 1. CULTURE IS CO-CREATED

If you think culture is a one-person job or you think you can have a "Chief Culture Officer"; if you think you can delegate culture, or just "get it done" like a project or a task on your to-do list, think again. Culture can never be created. It can only be *co-created.*

No one person is responsible for creating culture. Do you know why? Because culture exists, whether you create it or not. The people around you are always creating a feeling around being together, whether they try to or not.

Think about any event, party, class, or convention: It's always the attendees (plural) who co-create the feeling of that event. Therefore (and here's the exciting part), *if people consciously create their reality together, it will produce a noticeable change in the culture or feeling of being together.*

I remember taking my first class at Zappos to learn about their culture. Rather than telling us about the culture as we sat there and listened, the instructor first asked us, "What do you think the word culture means?" And we discussed it. Then the instructor asked, "What do you think Zappos culture is?" And again we discussed it. The class content itself was co-created. Next, rather than just learn about Zappos culture and go home, we formed teams and created projects to further develop the company's culture, and we executed them within the month.

(**Side note:** Just in that short story, did you read the values that were embedded within that experience? Can you recognize a culture that values open-mindedness, learning, and execution?

Values are not posters on a wall. Values are experienced every day whether you state them or not.)

Keep this in mind: *People value that to which they contribute.* (Say that to yourself a few times.) Imagine a dinner party where you and a group cooked together and took care of all the arrangements. I would bet you enjoyed that meal a lot more than if you had just shown up and everything had been prepared for you.

Now, think about any initiative regarding people — a class you want to teach, a project you want to start, a new interview process you want to use, a new policy to roll out. *How can it be co-created?*

If you can take that approach and roll with it, go for it. If you want more of a framework, gather a group and try this:

1. Take a step back and clearly define what you're doing and why.
2. Ask everyone what this initiative would ideally feel like on an emotional level.
3. Ask for their ideas on what can be done to co-create that experience. Let them speak more than you do.
4. Narrow down the ideas to the ones with the highest amount of leverage (Leverage = high ratio of output to the amount of energy put into it).
5. Ask who is passionate about which idea. Then ask for the passionate people to commit to a next action step in front of their peers.

Once you have co-created the culture, what strengthens it is sharing it...

## 2. SHARE WHAT YOU WANT TO KEEP

Sometimes people asked us at Zappos, "Why are you sharing your culture? That's your competitive edge!" Yes, that is true, but culture is people, and people can't be copied. So there's no reason to fear sharing it. In fact the opposite is true: The more culture is shared, the stronger it becomes.

As of this writing, 25,000 people come through the Zappos offices this year to simply watch people work. If anything, this sounds like a major distraction, right? So how can this make the culture stronger?

### Sharing inspires integrity and accountability.

When you share your culture, it's now on display. You can't hide it in the back of the room. So it becomes patently obvious whether or not you as an organization are living your own values. We tend to hold ourselves accountable when our work is on display. So why not be on display all the time?

### Sharing inspires appreciation.

As humans, we can take the greatest of pleasures for granted if we experience them every day. So what keeps things new? When visitors see other people watching them with wide-open eyes, wishing they could work there, then employees suddenly feel grateful because they remember that the rest of the world is not like this.

### Sharing inspires a culture of giving.

When more and more people ask about your culture, or anything else about your business, it's an opportunity to give. It's an opportunity to enlighten. By making this activity a habit, it goes on throughout the organization. People become used to giving and sharing, and what people become used to becomes "the way things are done around here."

Other companies such as Netflix, Hubspot and Spotify are sharing their culture and management principles and techniques. For links to these, go to www.cultureblueprint.com/resources.

When you share the culture, you are actually providing the energy to keep it going, because...

### 3. CULTURE FEEDS ON CULTURE

What do you think it takes to perpetuate a strong culture? Oddly enough, it's culture itself.

What? How does that even make sense?

Follow this logic:

- Culture is a feeling, created by people.
- People come together through relationships.
- Relationships are built through communication.
- Communication is made up of stories (even commands have a story behind them)
- Stories are made of language.
- Thus everyday language creates the feeling.

So ultimately it's stories and language that are powering culture. The more you develop the language and the stories in your organization, the more you strengthen the culture.

Let's look at a few real world examples so that this makes sense. Imagine you have an event at work. People are having a great time. They love it. They're bonding and you think about what a great team you have. But how do you make it last? Facebook has practically created a billion-person nation-state on this principle: *You preserve it and share it.*

So that means pictures, videos, quotes, and time to talk about the event the next day. You capture the moment, and bottle the magic so that you can share it, relive it, and use it to inspire the next event that outdoes the previous one.

You can start right away. All it takes is the video app on your smart phone.

One of my favorite moments as manager was interviewing a new candidate for the team, and the candidate asked, "Why do you all like working here?" Then I absolutely loved hearing each team member describe what was so amazing about our team and our culture.

Do you have moments like these? What if you proactively built them into your rituals? Ask yourself:

1. How can we start preserving the good times and our history?
2. Who is passionate about this?
3. Who loves video and photography?
4. How can we take time to share memories and talk about why we love working here?

When you see how culture feeds itself in a never-ending loop, you start to see how it is actually composed of systems. So next, let's look at what a system actually is, because if we understand systems, we understand culture.

## 4. CULTURE IS COMPOSED OF SYSTEMS

(Warning: We're about to geek out.)
A system is an interconnected set of elements that is coherently organized in a way that achieves something. We tend to focus on the elements of any system to try to improve it. But it is actually the interconnections, or the relationships between elements, that define the outcomes of a system. In other words, it's what's invisible.

For example, if you walked into Zappos you would see every kind of personality, and you would think there was no way these people could get along. However, it was the interconnectedness between people that created the bond.

There are three parts to any system:

- Elements
- Interconnections
- Purposes

Elements are what are visible. Interconnections can't be seen. And here is the most interesting part: The purpose of a system is NOT deduced from stated goals. The purpose is deduced from the behavior of the system itself.

That means that it is not strategy that is guiding the system. The behavior of the system itself is guiding it. (Thus the famous quote, "Culture eats strategy for breakfast.") The behavior is driven by the interconnections. And if those change, the entire system changes.

Let's use a basic example to make the point. Imagine an American football game and all of its elements (players, field, ball, etc.). Now, keep all of those elements, but change the rules of the game (which is the invisible part that prescribes how the elements interact). Change the rules of the game to those of soccer. The new game would be completely different, even though all the same elements are present. We changed the rules of interconnection.

Because everything is interconnected, there is no such thing as a "separate system." We can work on a subsystem, but changing one system will affect the others. So let's say you want to change a policy across the company. That means your change will be affecting many subsystems. The most effective way to deal with the resistance of these subsystems is to find a way to align their goals, and show how the policy change will add a new dynamic that will allow those subsystems to grow.

The limiting factor in any system is the highest leverage point for growth. In other words, the biggest source of frustration provides the biggest opportunity. (See section "This is Frustrating!")

Systems with similar feedback structures produce similar behavior dynamics even though the systems *appear* completely different (that's why this model of culture works in so many different kinds of businesses).

The one system that is present in every culture (regardless of group size, nationality, business, etc.) is the one everyone knows about, but no one really knows how it works on a theoretical level.

*It's called a "game."*

## 5. CULTURE IS A GAME

Have you ever found yourself frustrated with people who don't seem to put in enough effort? Maybe they used to, but now they've stopped. Or maybe they exert themselves half the time, but seem to be completely unproductive otherwise. It's easy to put the entire responsibility on employees. It's also a trap to blame ourselves as managers for not being inspirational enough. But consider another option:

*The problem is a poorly defined game.*

First, let's define a game, which is well articulated in Jane McGonigal's book *Reality is Broken*. Games may or may not be fun, but they all have this in common:

1. A goal
2. A rule set
3. A way to keep score (or receive feedback)
4. Opt-in play (with no compulsion by others to play)

McGonigal claims that these properties directly stimulate the happiness centers of the brain, in part because this structure encourages "blissful productivity" leading to happy-brain chemical production.

On a very basic level, you can see this at Zappos as a whole:

1. A goal – Become the best service company in the world
2. A rule set – The Zappos Family Core Values
3. Feedback – Financial performance, happiness scores, Net Promoter Score
4. Opt-in – Pay people to quit the company to make sure employment is completely opt-in.

If you want to know whether you are in a healthy culture or an unhealthy culture, all you have to do is determine if there is a strong game at play:

| Healthy Game / Culture | Unhealthy Game / Culture |
|---|---|
| **Clear Goal**<br>Everyone knows the goal and they are all aligned for the same purpose. | **Fuzzy Goal**<br>Some understand it, others don't. Some are not even aware. |
| **Clear Rules**<br>Everyone knows the rules, so everyone can play fairly. Core values often serve as rules of behavior. | **Vague Rules**<br>Rules are not obvious or they are constantly changing. No core values have been established and communicated. |
| **Accessible Feedback**<br>Visual aids are used so everyone knows the score. Feedback is structured so that people know where they stand. | **No Feedback**<br>No institutionalized way to track progress or get/offer feedback. |
| **Opt-in**<br>Projects and meetings are voluntary and agreements are made clear before beginning. | **Mandatory / Forced**<br>Projects and meetings are mandatory, forcing people to do things they are not passionate about, thus creating a major energy drain. |

(You can see a more detailed example of a game in the "Induct and Initiate" section).

**Agreement is the lynchpin in culture.**
I can often diagnose the problem with a culture when it comes to their level of opt-in, and the explicit format is in agreements.

Leaders often assume they are getting agreement, but unless you have explicit confirmation, then there is only the illusion of agreement. Let's give a real world example.

Restaurants need to know about reservation cancellations because holding an open table that will not be filled can cost them money. Typically, a confirmation would sound like this, "We have you down for 4 at 7:30. Please give us a call if anything changes."

This, in actuality, is a demand. There is no explicit agreement. However, when restaurants change their language to "We have you down for 4 at 7:30. Would you please call us if anything changes?" PAUSE. They wait for answer. The patron then says, "Yes," and they are far more likely to call because they have given their agreement.

The same thing is happening in organizations every time someone is assigned work. Without explicit agreement, there is no clear commitment. Directly asking a question is the way to test for willingness. And if there is resistance then it begs further questioning: Would they feel guilty to say no? Do they not have the resources? Is there a sacrifice they would need to make? Get curious!

Now let's go back to the game.

Think about those situations in which you were frustrated with those unproductive employees. Did you create a clear, measurable goal? Did you establish the rules for creating it? Did you have a clear rule in your own management game for what was unacceptable versus what could be coached? Did you receive an express commitment, or did you assume that they opted in? And did you give them regular feedback as they went through the process so that they knew if they were on track?

Like any good sports game, the end result is not just the win, but also an epic story that gets passed down from generation to generation. And that's why...

## 6. THE STORY IS CURRENCY

If you want people on your team to value customer service, the least effective way to do this is to tell them that customer service is important. That seems counterintuitive, right?

For example, you're sitting in a bar with a friend, and a guy comes up to you and says, "Hey, my name is Joe and I'm a really cool guy. Let me tell you about all the reasons I'm really cool." How likely are you a) to believe him, and b) to care?

The same thing happens when managers call a meeting and start telling people what they should value. Many people do not like being told what to do, but stories are a way to bypass this process.

Stories are values-embedded narratives in which people can locate themselves, and thus decide for themselves. If I tell you a story about my father, you will inevitably start thinking about your father. As I talk about my values in the form of a story, then you will resonate with the values we share.

Odds are that the movies and stories that you like the most have a piece of you in them. So in the above scenario, if I were to tell you stories about my life, then I'm not telling you what to think. I'm simply sharing what's important and meaningful to me in a way you can understand it, and then it is up to *you* to decide if I'm a "cool guy."

Stories are fantastic as a medium because if they are constructed correctly, and it's the right audience, then they are an entertaining way to build a shared history. When we think about America, we know the "story" behind its founding. Take any major religion — there is a story behind it. The ideas and philosophies are embedded within, but it's the story that we remember and that *makes it easy to pass on to future generations.*

A great brand is a story that never stops unfolding. (For more on the intersection of story and brand, see www.getstoried.com.)

Like a currency, a story is a medium that contains value (in this case the value is actually the story's values). It can be transmitted and exchanged without any cost beyond the time it takes to tell it. That's why it's easier to share a story about great customer service and how it changed an employee's own life, rather than simply giving a directive that emphasizes how service is important.

Next you will learn most important currency that allows all other culture currencies to flow freely.

## 7. THE SECRET TO INNOVATION

Everyone wants innovation. But you actually may not be ready for a culture of innovation.

What do you think it is that drives innovation?

Let's bring it to the level of culture. What is the difference between an employee who takes initiative and makes ideas happen versus one who does not do anything? Yes, those with initiative are drivers, but the answer is not to simply hire drivers who will act independently. That's like recruiting an all-star team and expecting it to perform better than a seasoned team of players who have already learned to successfully intuit each other's every move and act as a group.

The reason why people don't take action is one word: Fear. This may seem obvious, but you may not realize how deep it goes. It may be hard to imagine, but this is the thought chain that goes through an employee's mind:

*If I take this action, I might step on someone's toes.*
*Or I might get it wrong.*
*If I get it wrong, I could hurt the company.*
*If I hurt the company, I might lose my job.*
*If I lose my job, I might not get work for another six months.*
*If I don't get paid, I wouldn't make my mortgage.*
*I'll have to move out.*
*I won't be able to pay for my kid's school.*
*My relationship with my spouse would deteriorate as well...*
*You know what, I'm just going to do what's in my job description instead.*

This is going on in almost every company, even the best.

What most people don't realize is that innovation is driven over a steady road called **safety.**

Yes, it is safety that underlies every culture of innovation. So innovation is not about how to run brainstorming meetings, whiteboards and off-sites. The answer is to create a culture of safety.

So how do you that? There's one way to find out. When is the last time you celebrated (not just tolerated) a failure?

When did you announce to the company, "Jonathan took a great idea and put it into action. He had a strong rationale for it. Unfortunately it resulted in a loss of customers, but we learned a great lesson in this. Thank you, Jonathan."

Is it on display that it is okay to fail?

**Note:** As with all complex adaptive systems, there is a latency effect here. People will not feel safe at first. It takes time to develop, but stick to it to show consistency.

# Chapter Two

## Lay the Foundation

## ○ DETERMINE YOUR MISSION

Have you ever been confused about an organization's mission or vision? Do you ever read mission and vision statements and think they sound the same? Or do you ever find their language so highfalutin that you immediately forget them?

These are all examples of mission and vision gone bad. Don't throw them out entirely just yet. Let's work through the example of how Zappos uses mission and vision and you can decide for yourself whether it's a tool you want to use.

## What is a mission?

The mission is the purpose of your business, and it never changes. The mission answers the question, "Why are we coming to work every day?"

The Zappos mission is to "Live and Deliver WOW!" Notice that it's simple, powerful, easy to remember, and invokes an emotion. Also notice that it addresses both the inside of the company (the employees) and the outside of the company (the customers).

Most missions only involve the customers (or people being served), but this is a terrible notion. Without taking care of your people, who will deliver? In order to take care of others, you *must* take care of yourself. That is why your own team's needs (not wants, but needs) come before the customers'.

Let's use another example. Consider a non-profit whose mission is to address poverty. Let's say their mission is "Fight Hunger." Do you see the issue here? It does not care for the people who are actually doing the fighting. And secondly, the word "fight" itself creates emotions of difficulty, danger, and violence.

Now consider if they change it to "Feed the world, and feed our souls." In this new mission the active verb is positive and evokes the emotion of taking care of people. It also addresses the idea of supporting the growth and advancement of the people doing the serving. This is an organization built to last, because it will consistently retain its people (instead of their "fighting" eventually tiring them out or scaring them off). Does this make sense?

## How to know your real mission

Here is the key question you can ask to get to your real mission, beyond the plaque on the wall: What business are you really in? Read that again: *What business are you really in?*

Zappos realized early on that it was not in the business of selling shoes. It all started with an obstacle, a limitation. Take yourself back to the late nineties, when people were hesitant to put their credit cards online to buy books, let alone shoes! Zappos had a major objection to contend with without the money to advertise on TV, the way all the dotcom companies did at the time.

Instead of competing, Zappos decided to play a different game. All the money that would have been spent on marketing was poured into the customer experience. This included faster shipping, more customer service agents, longer call times — anything to make Zappos something *worth telling people about*. No one knew if it would work, but at least it was a game they had a chance at winning.

Zappos not only had an early challenge acquiring customers, it had one with vendors as well. Since it was a new company, most big shoe brands would not sell to it — and this was in an industry in which brands were known for courting distributors. The company turned this obstacle into a great advantage: In creating a culture of service, they treated their vendors like gold too. Vendors were (and still are) considered the lifeline of the company. So Zappos always picks up the check, picks them up from the airport, helps them with their gear, and even throws a huge end-of-the-year party for them.

Through these challenges, Zappos discovered that service was its mission. And great service quickly led to product expansion, from shoes to clothing, accessories, handbags, and housewares, and then to consulting and training through Zappos Insights.

So rather than thinking about a mission statement, consider these questions:

- What game are you playing?
- What business are you really in?
- What business do you need to be in?

Write down a few ideas (do it now!).

As you drive home tonight, or to work tomorrow morning, don't turn on the radio and fill your mind with irrelevant news or music that gets stuck in your head, or make calls you don't have to make. Let the questions above (and others, as you continue to read) fill your head instead. I know this is strange, but just let them be there, in silence.

As your ideas come to you, don't write them down until you arrive at your destination. Keep thinking about them over and over, add new ones, and then go back to thinking about the old ones. They will build on each other and gradually become clearer.

It's easy to want to rush this process and reveal your newly created mission statement. But if a mission statement is answering the question "Why am I going to work every day?" isn't it worth significant time and consideration to come to a truthful answer?

# ○ CREATE YOUR VISION

The vision, while imagined, is meant to become very real. It may sound lofty, but it should be realized in two to five years because this is a time frame that your people can envision. It's enough time to accomplish something big, but not so far ahead that people might consider big career changes. Let me give you the examples from Zappos and then we'll break down exactly how it's done.

Vision 1 – Become the biggest shoe store in the world (done)
Vision 2 – Offer the best service in the world (done)
Vision 3 – Become the best place to work (top 10 by 2010)

Notice a few qualities about each of these visions:

• Achieved (or achievable) in 2-5 years
• Builds on and uses the resources acquired through the last vision
• Short, simple, easy to remember (no long, indecipherable pages)
• Inspiring

Here are a few criteria for a great vision:

• It serves the mission (purpose).
• There's a verifiable way to achieve it.
• It creates a larger context for the day-to-day work.
• People see themselves in the larger story.
• It builds on itself (past visions actually continue and evolve).
• There is a sense of drama created through the unknown (Meaning, we could fail, but that's what makes it interesting).
• Every level of employee is inspired.
• It makes even the most menial task worthy of excellence.

Here is a simple question you can ask to get to your vision:

*What would we do if we could do the impossible?*

Keep in mind, not everyone will love it, or even get it. But focus on those who do.

# ○ ESTABLISH YOUR VALUES

Now we are getting to the good stuff...

What is most important is the organization's values. Why? Because they are already operating and running the show — you just don't know it.

If you were to walk into any organization and then shrink and grow wings to become a fly on the wall, you would soon learn what it values by simply observing how people talk, what they spend their time doing, what gets covered in meetings, and most importantly, *what is considered of higher importance than anything else.* For example, you can tell if a company values efficiency over service, or profits over people.

Values are the DNA of any organization. And the good news is that they can be hacked. They can be re-engineered to create the outcome and experience you desire within your organization.

As we did with "culture," let's start by looking at the meaning of the word itself. (This is a great habit, because as we've said, language creates culture.) While the main definition we are using is the last in this upcoming list, the other definitions come into play:

**VALUE - noun**  /'valyo͞o/
values, plural

1. The regard that something is held to deserve; the importance or preciousness of something.
2. The worth of something compared to the price paid or asked for it.
3. The usefulness of something considered in respect of a particular purpose.

4. The relative rank, importance, or power of a playing card, chess piece, etc., according to the rules of the game.
5. A person's principles or standards of behavior; one's judgment of what is important in life.

# ● Why Values are Valuable

First, let's discuss the value of values.

You may already be convinced that core values are important. But that will not be enough to go through the process of discovering core values, conveying your passion to others, and ultimately aligning the entire company around them. This introduction has been created to arm you with the inspiration and the reasoning for either starting the core values process or simply reinforcing what you have already created.

Why create core values?

**1. Values make the decisions.**
Values provide a decision-making framework. There are many ways to reach any goal, but the values prescribe what is acceptable versus unacceptable. The result is that the values themselves start to "manage" people because they mark boundaries. These boundaries create a container in which self-organization is possible. Without boundaries (or with unclear boundaries) any decision can be justified, chaos ensues, and a high level of policing is then required to maintain order.

Without core values, there is no solid structure for decision-making. Without this framework, people resort to likes and dislikes, gut feelings, or — even worse — decisions are made out of fear of getting it wrong. The core values provide a set of guidelines that help people make decisions.

When boundaries are clear, it's easy for anyone to take responsibility and say, "Wait, that's not right." The organization, in a sense, becomes a healthy immune system that will automatically eject something (or someone) that is a threat to the health of the overall system.

The reason this works is due to a concept that Dan Mezick, author of *The Culture Game*, calls "loose constraints with high integrity." This means that the value itself is not prescribed with exact behaviors. That said, everyone understands what it means, and that the organization is willing to let go of any person who does not adhere to the values.

Values are the key ingredient to building an organization that lasts beyond its visionary charismatic founder. Values outlive goals, trends, strategies, and even people.

When the values are truly unique to the organization, and they are followed with strict integrity, *the outside world must adjust to the organization.*

Yes, you read that correctly. If your values are unique to you, and you adhere to them with no compromise, then you will be shaping your world, and the rest of the world will have to deal with you.

Here's how that worked for Zappos. The company committed to such a high level of service that even in the face of lower profits, their service level was their chief priority. And now, as a result, many online retailers have changed their policies (such as providing free shipping and direct phone service) because, thanks to Zappos, consumers now have come to demand it.

### 2. Values create a self-managed organization.

Values mean leadership is distributed. When you hire people with similar core values, you bring people who already resonate with the culture, and they naturally have the behaviors and attitudes (and thus actions) that ultimately drive results.

When the values (boundaries) are clear, it's easy to see who is the right fit in the organization and who is not. Values attract the right people and repel the wrong people (and that includes customers).

### 3. Values create the experience you want.

All business today is about creating experiences. Why? Because we are all in the business of communication. Almost your whole day is spent on email, phone calls, meetings, reading, writing, researching, presenting, or selling — all forms of communication, which is based on relationships. And we pick our relationships based on the experiences we want to have with people. By committing to core values, we are committing to the experience that drives results, rather than to the results themselves.

### 4. Values outlive goals, trends and people.

People have asked if the Zappos culture would survive if CEO Tony Hsieh was not here. Did Disney survive without Walt? Disney's values (in order of priority) are safety, show, courtesy and efficiency. They pass the culture onward.

However, history is filled with companies who had great leaders, but once the leaders left, the companies failed. Creating a culture that lasts means developing a system that transcends all leaders. A system based on solid core values can continue indefinitely. Leadership comes and goes.

### Why does setting values work so well?

It's the concept of loose constraints with high integrity. Loose constraints means values can be interpreted. People may have different views of them, which creates diversity that keeps the organization strong, and adaptive.

So what keeps it from going into chaos? How does the system stay resilient but faithful to the original intentions of the core values? This is done by setting expectations of high integrity around the values so that everyone knows how serious the company is about them.

| Loose Constraints **AND** High Integrity | |
| --- | --- |
| Very few rules (instead of large rule books). | Hire by values, fire by values. |
| Values are open to interpretation. | Value integrity is treated as greater in importance than performance factors. |
| Assumes people are adults and need inspiration rather than micromanagement. | Small violations are taken through a warning process. Large violations lead to immediate termination. |

### Values are at play, whether you realize it or not.

We are always acting in accordance with what we value. We simply may not be conscious of it. For example, someone may say they value their health, but eat terribly. What is actually true is they value freedom and the ability to do whatever they want, more than they value their health.

In Zappos customer service, team members will occasionally make policy exceptions to enhance the customer experience. This does not mean that the team members do not value the policies, but they can't predict every situation, and the value "Deliver WOW! through service" may require breaking a policy (and having management potentially re-evaluate it).

### The true test of values

Here is the test for whether a company is really living by its values:

1. Leadership lives them (and it's obvious).
2. The company hires by them and fires by them.
3. The values are used as decision-making criteria.

This last one means that an employee can challenge any decision maker (regardless of position) if they believe a decision is in violation of one of the core values. In fact, if they do not object then it is harmful to the culture, so they must actually be encouraged.

## ● The Magic Formula

Here is the formula to turn values into action:

1. Set a standard (Standard = Value + Unwillingness to compromise).
2. Make a bold promise (both to your customers and to your people).
3. Deliver on that promise (regardless of market conditions).

This is the simple process to create a world-changing organization that no one would ever want to leave. And customers are willing to pay a higher price for a standard they can count on.

When Zappos decided to value service, it set the standard as "WOW!" This meant not just good, or even great, service — it had to be something so incredible that people were shocked by it.

The bold promise (very revolutionary at the time) was to ship shoes the very next day.

However, to deliver on that promise, the company had to control the entire process of getting boxes to UPS. This was impossible for the brands that would only ship out on behalf of Zappos. So there was a choice: Keep the selection broad, with many brands, or cut those brands (along with the revenue) and only work with those companies that would allow Zappos to control the customer experience. The company dropped 25 percent of their brands in one day, and it produced a drastic reduction in revenue.

Many said that it made no economic sense. But in the long run, the brand changed the service standards for all e-commerce companies. But most importantly, customers loved it, and Zappos became the biggest shoe store in the world.

Before you can determine your bold promise and deliver on it, first you need to know your values. Let's get into the process of how to do that. First, you want to make sure you're focused on clear values over vague values.

# ● Types of Values

In both working with companies on their values and in analyzing the values of very successful companies I found a meta-structure to the types of values they use.

### 1. Key Differentiator Values
These are values that distinguish the company from any other, and also help them lead the field. For Zappos it's the WOW! service and the weirdness to its culture. For Apple it's design and excellence. For Google it's the top academic performance and engineering.

### 2. Supporting Values
These are the values that are supportive of the vision and the key differentiator. They include learning, growth and others that are not directly connected to the business model.

### 3. Experience Values

These are the values that guide what kind of experience a company would like to have, regardless of the state of the business. They can include adventure, fun, etc.

### 4. Über Values

These are the values that must be present, otherwise the other values will not work. They include integrity (because what good is any other standard if a person has no integrity), willingness (because anything forced will ultimately not work), and relevance (because if people cannot see why a value, goal or assignment is relevant, it will be dismissed).

### 5. Defensive Values

These are values that people include because they are actually defending against something else. When people include "respect" as a value, it's often to try to prevent terrible experiences that have happened in the past. Also, "honesty" without context (or the "why") is a defensive value. I recommend thinking about these and making sure the wording you use is very proactive instead of defensive.

## ● Clear Values vs. Vague Values

Not all values are created equal. Some are stronger than others. We will get into the exact process for how you can create values, but first let's think about this at a higher level.

Why does the plaque on the wall with values such as "Honesty, Integrity and Teamwork" seem to mean absolutely nothing at all? Where do I even begin?

First, these words can mean so many different things to different people. The word honesty (to some) will simply convey that leadership is concerned that people are stealing from the company.

Also, is honesty always good? If I go around the company telling people what I really feel, will that create a great environment? No. You can easily ruin someone's day just by being honest with no care or consideration. Without more context, this is an example of a weak value.

Let's take a look at the way Zappos deals with the value of honesty. The specific value is:

"Build open and honest relationships through communication."

Notice a few things about it. First, the priority in the statement is the relationship. Everything in this sentence is there to support people's relationships. Second, it's not one word, it's a complete sentence that clearly articulates the purpose of the value. Lastly, it starts with a verb, meaning it's actionable. And (I'm giving you a preview of what's to come), what you don't see is:

a) **Documentation** of the core values to explain what they mean
b) **Examples** of the company's history of living them
c) **Stories** from individuals given to every training class explaining how the particular core value changed their lives.

But as I said, we're getting ahead of ourselves because first we need to understand values at a mechanical level. Before we get into the exact technique for how to create them, consider the following questions:

- What causes the value and what beliefs are necessary?
- What will happen if we do this, or do not do this? (consequences)
- How will we know that the value is in action? (evidence)

# ● Optimize Your Values

Optimization in a culture is all about selecting the value that leads the other values.

To continue with an architecture metaphor, a building's structure is designed differently for a small business, a large business, a private family, a social family, a sports family, etc. In that same way, building a culture should have a focus. This is what we call *optimization.*

You can tell what a culture is truly optimized for by having someone visit for a day and then having them complete this sentence: "The people here are really all about _____."

So for example, Zappos is optimized for service (To learn more about the full list, just Google "Zappos core values"). This value runs throughout every aspect of the organization. Apple is optimized for excellence, Google is optimized for engineering.

Any optimization does come with its trade-offs, though. A high-service organization requires a lot of energy as well as a very social and outgoing group. If you're shy and unsocial, you won't do well there. Apple's culture of excellence will not be very nice for someone who likes to lead a relaxed lifestyle; the first sign of this you might see may be when you walk in to the office and someone is talking about how they worked over the weekend.

Here are a few more effects of optimization to consider:

- A culture optimized for collaboration will have slower response times, and less targeted efforts.
- A culture optimized for discipline will not have a lot of hugging, peace-loving hippies.

- A culture optimized for self-management will require a *lot* of meeting time to keep people abreast of the information they need to do their jobs.

You may even notice that values in your own life are probably already optimized. For example, my life is optimized for learning successful models of mindsets and behaviors, putting them into action, and training others to do this as well. Another person's life may be centered on providing as a mother.

It seems that more and more of the most successful organizations are focused on organizational learning. As the rate of change increases in any industry, the learning organizations will be the quickest to respond.

## ● The Mindset Model

So why put such a big focus on values? Because they are at the center of all change:

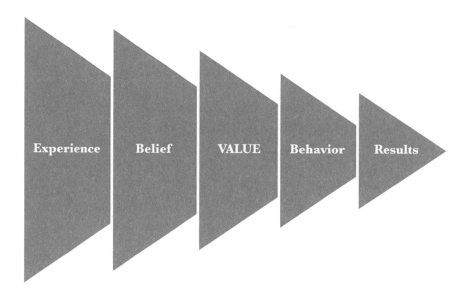

Experience | Belief | VALUE | Behavior | Results

Simply looking at results, actions, and behaviors will not create lasting change because they are driven by underlying values. Values are created after an experience that programs our beliefs, which then inform our values.

Beliefs are the bridge between assumptions and results. We believe that if we do X, then we will get Y result. And we learn this through our own experiences, with past bosses, as customers of other businesses, and even our own parenting or childhood. These beliefs are what inform our values and they can rarely be changed, unless through a powerful experience. This is why the attraction process you will read about in coming chapters is all about pulling in people who share your values.

Once those values are set, the behaviors and actions create new results that lead to an experience of the values in action that further solidifies and reinforces the values.

## ● The Core Value Discovery Formula

Now keep in mind that discovering and creating values is not something that gets done and wrapped up in a weekend. Why? Because you're going to commit to these values for life. (The Zappos core values have never changed.)

Think about it like dating. If you're serious, you're not going to get married after one date. Your core values need to be mulled over. Play around with them, socialize with them, test them against real situations and people.

### 1. Commit to running a core values-based company.

This first step is vital. This is the commitment to running the company to a standard that goes beyond goals, people, investors, and profits. This is about committing to a structure that will take your organization from good to great. This is about making decisions for the long term, even when they may be painful in the short term — even resulting in losses. The benefit is having an organization that almost runs itself.

Are you willing to commit to running a core values-based company?

### 2. Determine your personal values.

It can be surprisingly hard, but it's important to know what you, as a leader, consider most important. Your own core values do not have to be the same as the company's, but they must be in alignment. There's a simple way to do it, though to be thorough, it takes an investment of time. Think about your best moments in life. As you look at those experiences, ask yourself, what values were present? Now think about your worst moments. What values were absent? Think about movie scenes where you were moved to tears or chills. What values were present there?

### 3. Determine key people's personal values.

Think about the people who fully embody the culture you desire. Think about the values they embody, and also ask them what they believe their values are.

### 4. Combine the discovered values.

Notice the trends, see what words can be combined. Come up with a list of thirty or less.

### 5. Test the values.

Ask managers to see if those values are in alignment with those of their best employees or ex-employees.

### 6. Test your commitment.

Are you willing to hire and fire based on whether an employee fits these core values? Would you hire a culture non-fit for a short-term gain?

## 7. Send the list to the entire company and ask for feedback.

Please don't use a committee to make the final decision. Committees and groups are great for ideas and feedback, but when it comes to making a decision, it's on the leaders.

Also remember, you can't make everyone happy, and that's a good thing. When Zappos chose "Create fun and a little weirdness," it actually turned off many people and some left as a result. So when you have a finished set of values, think about what delivery method will be most impactful and persuasive, whether it is an email or a company-wide meeting.

## 8. Change the list to uniquely worded values.

When creating unique values, try to make them statements instead of just single words (e.g., "Deliver WOW! Through Service" and "Build a Positive Team and Family Spirit.") Take the words that you have chosen, and write down what they mean to you. Choose words that would inspire you to get up every morning. Start with verbs, so that you put them into action. Limit the total to ten or less.

## 9. Roll out the values to the entire company.

Making the big announcement about your new values is crucial. There are many ways you can disseminate information, whether it is through emails, individual team meetings, or a company quarterly meeting. The point is that you should be showing a public commitment, and not just once but often, on an ongoing basis.

## 10. Integrate the core values into everything you do.

Take a look at your processes, one by one, to see how you can integrate your core values. But don't take this on alone. Remember, co-creation is the core of culture development. Crowd-source this step of the process so that each department comes up with ideas. Don't try to do it all at once. It's not a race and you don't want to overwhelm your teams. If you think it is going to be difficult to implement change, start small. We'll cover more on integration in the next sections.

<u>To summarize:</u>
The "Why?" is your mission.
The "What?" is your vision.
The "How?" are your values.

# ● Aligning the Core Values

Below are general principles for aligning your core values. Since there are so many specific ways to do this, you can read about techniques in the "Culture Toolkit" chapter.

### Share them.

Culture is expressed in and transmitted by language. Start talking about your core values on a regular basis. Include them in company updates, meetings, emails, and side conversations. Consider starting a blog about them (It will keep you very accountable). Get them into every touchpoint with your employees and customers.

### Create feedback mechanisms.

Without feedback, everything is a one-way message. Make sure you have ways for people to provide open and honest communication. Open up channels for people to ask questions and provide ideas. Then transmit the feedback back to the company, communicate what action is being taken, and open up opportunities for volunteers to step in.

### Teach them.

One of the fastest ways to learn is to teach someone else to understand or do something. Consider how you can educate others about what you're learning about your values and culture. It can be as simple as a brown-bag lunch with co-workers. If you help others to understand what you're learning, it will resonate with you at a much deeper level.

### Empower departments and subcultures.

As a leader, it's not your job to change the culture. It's your job to articulate your vision and values clearly, select the right people, and then empower them to do what they do best. Now that you have your core values, let the departments run with them. Challenge them to think about each value in relation to every one of their processes. Teams and departments will have different styles, which is fantastic as long as they all agree on the core values. Let them each do things differently so they can express their passions.

### Evaluate by them.

How can values be the criteria by which you evaluate the success of your people?

### When in doubt, start a conversation.

As a leader, one of your growth areas will always be empowering others. In fact, the best leaders often have a lot of free time because great decisions and great hires are not correlated with an eighty-hour workweek.

So if you find yourself with some spare time (or blocked, or frustrated), simply start a conversation. It's best to do it in a triad because you'll build the relationship between two other people. Allow yourself to be surprised with the wisdom that comes as a result — as long as you are clear on your vision and your commitment to the core values.

Here's an example of how to keep the values alive (and reduce your management headaches at the same time). Let's say that you're concerned about the spending activity of a person or department, and you have the core value "Do more with less." The temptation in the moment is to simply be critical or go for an interrogation. (e.g. Why are you spending money on this? Are you really being efficient?) But the emotions that you will trigger will be fear and resentment. Yes, you'll get an answer, but you'll disrupt all the great work you did to establish a strong culture.

Instead, let the value itself become the trigger (which will bring back all those stories as well as the great times they had through training). *That way it's not about personal dislikes or politics. It's about the values to which all are committed.*

So you could say, "I'd like to talk about how we can do more with less on the recent spending." This is something you have both signed on to do, so your people should be willing and able to have such a conversation. Or you can put the work on them and offer it as a question: "What is your approach to doing more with less?"

# ● Navigating the Core Pitfalls

If you're having any problems rolling out the core values, you can diagnose it back to one or several of these reasons:

**1. Commitment** – Are you fully committed? Is your team fully committed? Have they sworn an oath or signed a contract? How can you be sure everyone is fully committed?

**2. Clarification** – Is it clear what the values are and what they mean? Have you written out a document with examples, stories, and specifications of what it means to live out these values?

**3. Communication** – Does everyone really know what the core values are? Have they been discussed in smaller groups? Have they read the documentation? Consider a fun way to have people start talking about them, and conjuring up ideas on how to apply them.

**4. Conversation** – Are people using them in everyday conversation? Are you? Practice speaking from the place of the values. Use them in key decision-making processes. Bring them up at the beginning of meetings as a way to focus the conversation. Play games based on memorizing the values.

# ● The True Values Test

It all comes down to this: Are you willing to fire someone who does not fit the values, despite their performance?

You know you are truly committed when you are willing to hire and fire by the values of the company. This means that if someone is a great performer but they do not meet every value, then you must not bring them on board. And if they violate a core value, you must be willing to terminate their employment, immediately.

This is what separates the followers from the leaders. Most managers can't stand to lose a star performer, but if that person is toxic to the culture, then they can ultimately bring down the company. It takes years to build up a reputation; it takes only one bad move to completely ruin it.

# Chapter Three

## Design the Blueprint

## ○ INTRODUCING THE BLUEPRINT

As mentioned earlier, *The Culture Blueprint* is a system that starts with a simple vague notion of what you want, and ends with a system of culture running so well that it can operate on its own. For that reason, you don't have to worry about using the entire blueprint all at once. In fact, you may already be halfway there.

Keep in mind that this is a different kind of blueprint. It will actually be designed as you are developing the culture. The blueprint is more of a map that allows you to see where you are in the process, and to make sure you're taking everything into account. You may actually re-order the map.

It's key to get this concept: *You cannot design culture.* You can only design the frameworks around the culture. And you cannot create culture either: You can only co-create it. I cannot stress this enough. If you're working alone, then you're working too hard.

The blueprint might feel overwhelming. There are a lot of moving parts, but it is also a fractal model. What that means is that you can work on any part of it and it will actually have an effect on all the other parts.

The most important part is **movement**. *Studying will not shift your culture. It is only conversation and action that will do it.* So just know, if you find yourself taking a long time to read through this book, then you're already behind. The blueprint is designed *as* you're building the culture.

So don't spend too long here, as the blueprint itself will not completely make sense until you're fully into it. As you'll see, it's all about experimentation.

# ● The Culture Blueprint

**INSPIRATION**

 "I have to address this, NOW!"

**THE CULTURE HERO**

You

**THE IMMERSION**

 "I've experienced a great culture. I see how great this can be."

**VISION**

My Vision

**BOLD ACTION STEP**

Bold Action Step

**THE CULTURE CREW**

Mentor/Coach    Help!    Culture Crew

**THE CULTURE GROWTH ENGINE**

Attract & Repulse › Induct & Initiate › Serve & Deliver › Engage & Sustain › Share & Observe

## INSPIRATION

 ”I have to address this, NOW!”

Shifting your organization's culture *starts with your reason why.* Why are you reading this book? What motivated you? Sometimes it's a friend, or an article, or a pressing need for change, or the sense that something could be better. It could be a number of things, but it always starts with inspiration.

You've already hit that step, so why mention it? Because if you plan to enroll others in your mission, they will need inspiration as well, and their inspiration may look different from yours. In order to understand what any sponsor, manager, boss, or investor cares about, you must listen to them carefully; only then will you be able to convey your message to them in their language and truly be of service.

## THE CULTURE HERO

 You

**Become the culture hero.**
"Who me?" you ask. Yes, you. You don't have to be a manager, or a leader, or even someone with any influence at all. It's you because you care, and because you're willing — that's really all it takes to be a culture hero. This book is here to guide you through the rest.

The word "hero" is used here in reference to Joseph Campbell's work on the mono-myth — the unifying storyline that runs through every great tale from *The Odyssey* to *Star Wars.* It's an effective model because it involves both personal fulfillment and transformation as well as the mission of helping a larger group or community. It's also an encouraging model because every story makes clear that the hero was initially *unqualified*. The hero had never done this before, *but the journey itself turned him or her into a person who could.*

In the team section, we will start with the philosophies, principles, and exercises you can do to prepare yourself for this journey.

## THE IMMERSION

 "I've experienced a great culture. I see how great this can be."

### Immerse yourself in culture.

Immersion means a direct experience in the world you would like to create. At Zappos Insights, we learned this lesson very early on. We created a two-day boot camp event with the intention of capturing it on video and sharing the content through the website. The event was a smashing hit. And considering all the smiling faces we saw, when we asked for feedback, we honestly expected people to say that our content blew their minds. Instead they replied, "The content was good, but we knew most of it from reading all about Zappos. It was the experience of being here that really changed everything. Now I really believe it's possible."

So consider what experiences you've already had, and ones you would like to create, and immerse yourself and your team in a powerful experience.

**VISION**

## My Vision

**Create your vision.**

Vision is much simpler than people realize. You read in the previous chapter all about how to create a powerful, effective vision that gets people into action. A vision is an image of what you want to achieve, not in a lifetime, but within a few years. A vision is short, memorable, and powerful, and people can see where they fit into it.

Examples include:

- "Create the biggest _____ in the world."
- "Develop a culture on the Fortune 100 Best Places to Work."

These are overarching company visions. But you can create a smaller vision that can be accomplished much more quickly.

For example:

- "Create quarterly celebrations of all we have accomplished."
- "Convert our office into an expression of who we are."
- "Develop an on-boarding process (how you bring people into the company and train them) so that people take full ownership of the culture."

After you have an inspiring vision, next you will have to prove to yourself that you really can do this, and also show others you are serious.

## BOLD ACTION STEP

# Bold Action Step

### Take a bold action step.

This is the threshold, the test that says, *"You know what, you can stay where you are and be comfortable. Or you can try something new. It's risky. You may not be able to go back. But what's the cost of staying where you are?"*

One boot camp participant realized that the risk was actually an illusion:

*"After returning from the Boot Camp Immersion at Zappos, I had a vision for what our culture could be like. I told a lot of people above me, but they didn't feel we could do it. I felt like leaving the company. And then I realized, if I'm willing to quit over this, why don't I just give it a shot? So I started making changes without even having permission."*

(We will go into many simple but bold action steps you can take within the "Immediate Wins" section.)

One of the first actions she took was to put up stats of her department's performance on the walls. Doesn't sound like a big risk, right? Except that the CEO had said not to put anything on the walls!

"I was proud of all that we'd done and I wanted everyone to see our numbers," she said. People at her company loved it. Even the IT department asked if they might replace it with an LCD screen that could show live updates. The CEO didn't even remember having told people not to put up things on the wall. And that small act of rebellion started a revolution. It set her up perfectly for the next step.

## THE CULTURE CREW

### Find your culture crew or mentor.

Her next step was to create the "Executive Culture Council." Never mind that she was not an executive! She put up signs for it, limited the number of people, and made them apply. What resulted was an amazing opt-in team of super-heroes for her to work with on the next, bigger project.

The other option (or additional option) is enlisting a mentor. A mentor may come in at any stage, and be inside or outside the organization, but when you recognize this person, take the opportunity to connect with him or her. (I once had a mentor who was a homeless person!). You will recognize the mentor as someone who has the information, experience, or the right questions that will arm you for success. Once this stage is complete, we have a foundation upon which to build.

## THE CULTURE GROWTH ENGINE

The culture growth engine is the key to developing, scaling, and maintaining a strong culture. The engine itself came out of a frustration shared by both me and my clients. Many people find shifting an organization's culture overwhelming: They learn about everything and have no idea where to start. This is the path that starts with the highest leverage points in the system and goes from there.

# ○ ATTRACT AND REPULSE

It all starts with the right people. With a strong culture, you will attract the right people, and repulse the wrong people. Even at Zappos, which has been called "Disneyland" by guests and co-workers alike, there are people who find it's really not for them. They don't like having a "weird" culture every day, or they find it too social, or without enough structure.

When you try to make your company attractive to everyone, you'll ultimately fail to get the right people in the door. But if you're clear on who you *are and who you are not,* then you'll get the right people, and many of the wrong people won't even show up.

That's the value of having core values that are very unique to your culture.

This process is typically called recruiting, but since that's based on a military model, we're playing with new language. Attraction is what happens when recruiting is going so well that the talent comes to you.

To extend the metaphor, it's like flirting. Can you imagine if you met someone, and after the first date they asked you to marry them? That is essentially what is happening when companies hire quickly. The new model is about being slow to hire because you're looking for a long-term commitment.

The attraction stage involves applications, interviews, screening, and involving the entire organization in the hiring process. This section will show you how to select the right people, lose the wrong people, and upgrade those in between.

# ● Job Descriptions

### Start with the wish list.

Think about everything you want in a candidate. What would be his or her ideal behavior, skills, demeanor, type of creativity? Ultimately, let's face it, you probably won't get someone who has everything you want. But at least you then know what you're training for.

### Create a powerful job description.

Here is a job description I wrote while running an online community for self-development. Rather than focusing entirely on what we needed, I first created a vision for what their day would be like at the company:

---

### Here's what a typical day might look like:

1. You drive to our office, most likely listening to a great book on CD to keep learning (or great music to get you pumped up). You get to the office and jump right on the site to see who's commenting. You send several welcome-emails, comment on the new posts, and answer people's questions, all with a great friendly tone and articulate language. You churn out the messages, and everyone on the site is relieved to have you there, singing your praises. (Someone proposes a parade in your honor, but they're all talk.)

2. After the morning, you look at your notes and talk to the community director about trends on the site, how we can improve the experience, and ways we can offer better help.

---

3. You head to lunch in the break room, joking around with the crew, laughing so hard that your VitaminWater comes out your nose.

4. Lunch is making you a bit sleepy, so you go to jump on the mini-trampoline for several minutes, perhaps while listening to "Eye of the Tiger" on your iPod.

5. After an afternoon of more comments and responses, you switch gears and contribute a story about how you overcame what seemed like an impossible situation, balanced by a lighter blog post about when you choked on a tofu skewer and managed to get a date with the person who gave you the Heimlich maneuver.

6. Midway through writing the story, a crisis comes up. Never one to panic, you stop typing and confidently say, "I'm on it!" like you're Bruce Willis taking on Russian terrorists in Die Hard.

7. Crisis solved. You shoot off a few emails telling a few friends or colleagues about some posts they might like, and then wrap up and head home. This time you drive in silence, thinking about the people who are really putting it out there to change their lives — the ones who have had enough, the ones who want more, the ones who are not afraid to create their own happiness, and...all the crazy and wacky ones that every online community has! You laugh to yourself and then think, "How might I help them out tomorrow?"

8. Are you ready for this? This is an opportunity with a high potential to grow. And to grow big, one must start small. Our starting compensation is $1,400 per month.

Yes, that was the budget I was given. And we actually got someone great (and then gave him a raise).

Another technique you can use is video. Again, this one may be over the top, but it's just to give you ideas:

www.worldsmostawesomejob.com

Every touchpoint is an opportunity to define your culture, and a job description is often the very first experience a new hire will have with your company.

# ● Interview Process

### Set useful application guidelines.

"The way you do one thing is the way you do everything," tends to be a truism about people's behaviors, so the application process is a way to see into how someone operates. Consider posing a challenge in your job descriptions. Sometimes it can be as simple as asking an applicant to respond with a very specific subject line in their email. That way you can immediately sort out who is good at paying attention to detail and following instructions.

At the other extreme, you may go so far as to require a short video to be submitted with the application. If you do, make sure to provide some basic guidelines, such as desired length and what you're looking for. Also let them know what you value. Aside from video production jobs, your judgment of them will not be about the video's production quality, so let them know that as well.

### Ask high-leverage questions.

Another way to sort through applications is to use high-leverage questions during the attraction process. These are questions that can give you a lot of information about a person without using up much of your time or theirs.

One great question comes from the book *The Luck Factor* by Richard Wiseman. This book explains how people who feel they are lucky are generally happier, more appreciative, and easier to get along with. On the other hand, people who do not feel they are lucky tend to feel entitled, that they are on their own, and that they are the only ones to credit for their own success. So the high-leverage question is:

*"How lucky do you feel you are, on a scale from 0 to 10?"*

You can also use questions that are related to your core values. So, for example, in relation to the Zappos core value "Create fun and a little weirdness," Zappos asks (in a live interview):

*"How weird are you on a scale from 0 to 10?"*

There is no right answer (although a 0 or a 10 certainly gives one pause and begs further questioning). The point is more to see how someone reacts to the question.

**Ask focused interview questions.**

You can ask questions to ascertain whether or not the candidate displays the corresponding desirable attributes and attitude. For example, if you want to hire someone who values service, you can say, "Tell me a time when you went out of your way to help a co-worker." In other words, take value, then form a story-based question to determine if they live (and enjoy it). More questions like these are available at www.ZapposInsights.com.

Interviewers can also "call an audible" by "improv"-ing questions. For example, if an interviewer thinks the person may be too uptight for the culture, the interviewer can ask, "What's your favorite swear word?" Followed up with "Please use that word in your next answer." Again, there is no right answer; it's more about how the person reacts to the question.

**Value culture over performance.**

Your general rule of thumb should be that culture trumps performance. People can make their record of performance look better than it is, but if you design a core values-based culture interview, it's hard for them to fake it. Also, you can often train for the skills you need, but you can't train someone on values — they either value something or they don't. That's why the value of "growth and learning" is so effective. People who value learning enjoy learning new skills (and thus learn quickly). People then grow into roles they were previously never qualified to take on.

**Always look to see the full person.**

Another powerful question is "If you could get paid to do anything, what would it be?" When Phil So answered this question, he said he would love to produce music. The interviewer replied, "Maybe you'll do that one day at Zappos." But Phil was incredulous. He was applying for a graphic designer position. One day he worked with the audio/video team to create a music video using his music. It was shown to the whole company and everyone loved it. As the company needed more audio for commercials and internal videos, he was offered a music producer role and even created an album of songs from musicians within the company.

You want people to feel free to bring their whole selves to work, because you never know when their interests and talents may be helpful. Also, when people are discouraged from bringing their interests and personalities to work, they tend to spend too much energy trying to fit.

### Say no to candidates.

Saying no can actually be a great experience. Whenever I have reached out to let a candidate know that we would not be interviewing them based on their application, I have always been surprised to receive emails back that say, "Thank you *so* much for getting back to me. I have sent out so many résumés and it's nice to hear that you reviewed it and took the time to let me know."

People appreciate being treated like people, and if you can make sure to thank them for applying and wish them good luck when you tell them no, it will only help your brand.

### When you say yes, make it unique, fun, and rewarding.

Of course a candidate will be glad to hear a "yes" regardless of how you say it, but how can you make this a memorable experience, and a bookmark in their lives? Consider shooting a quick video of your team feeling excited at the new hire's arrival. Or consider sending them a fun, welcoming care package with their acceptance letter.

# ○ INDUCT AND INITIATE

Once you've selected the right people, it's time to bring them into the organization in such a way that they understand the culture and their role in it and achieve that ultimate objective — they feel like they are part of the story and have a sense of pride and ownership.

No one knows this better than the military, who completely break down people's identities in the first few weeks of boot camp, then build them back up. Marching around may seem completely archaic, but it's a brilliant (and very inexpensive) tool to literally get people in sync with their bodies, their words, and their thoughts. Nothing suggested here will even come to close to such extremes. I only mention it to highlight the power of a good initiation.

Even if you've hired the right people, initiating them into the company is a totally separate process. It should ensure that they not only know how to do their jobs, but also know how to get what they need to support the entire organization. You know it's going well when new people feel that they've taken ownership. You know you've knocked it out of the park when they say they feel like they've come home.

Whether you have a day or a month to get someone in the door, there are systematic steps to follow so that you won't leave this important stage to chance.

## ● Induct Into the Organization

Inducting someone into your culture is a very big deal. You are letting them into your home and into your family and trusting them with all you have. But it's amazing to see how lightly most organizations take this. People's first day at work is usually limited to being given a desk and then shown where the bathroom and supply closets are. What a missed opportunity! As the saying goes, you never have a second chance to make a first impression.

At Zappos, they started inducting new staff with a daylong orientation, and now it has become a four-week adventure. Everyone goes through the customer service training from the CEO on down.

Before we get into the detailed breakdown, let's discuss some of the general benefits of crafting an extensive group orientation that will be a truly memorable experience:

- On-boarding with a group means that all new hires have a whole new set of best friends. This is important because the social pressures of being part of a new organization can sometimes be more stressful than the job itself.

- Presenting the history of the organization creates a sense of pride and appreciation for those who created this opportunity.

- Creating a challenging and rigorous on-boarding process (without guaranteed final admittance) makes for a powerful experience where people must be dedicated to the mission, work together, and hold themselves accountable to each other. These are some of the most important skills, and ones you cannot teach simply through information.

Now let's go over the structure of the training program itself. In each case, the content in parentheses shows how each step is a feature of game design.

**Introductions** (Character development)
Have the trainers introduce themselves by sharing their stories about how they came to the company and how their lives changed as a result. This will inspire the new hires to share their own stories. Have

them get to know each other by playing a game where they get a new nickname (new identity as part of a new group).

Zappos developed a process to build accountability: New hires are informed that they must arrive by 7am every day, or they would be cut from the program (rules for how your "avatar" — or game identity — can be killed). It's important to note that the program itself is co-created in real time. While instructors state the expectations of the company, new hires are asked for their expectations of what the company will provide them. Throughout the learning and exercises, new hires are asked for their opinions, and how they define the core values.

### History (Epic story)

Each new hire then learns about the history of the company. At Zappos, one can't help but feel a sense of pride after becoming a part of this world-changing company, and also because they know that only 2 percent of applicants are accepted.

### Core values (Story line, Rules)

Each core value is explained by someone from within the company (not a trainer). They talk about how the core value itself changed their life. Usually, as I've mentioned, values seem like staid words on a wall, but when you hear actual stories about them, they suddenly become real and actionable. In my own initiation, I was moved by talks in which the speaker was in tears explaining what a difference the values made.

### Training (Power development, Environment)

Consider what the core skill is that everyone must have. For example, at Zappos, everyone must learn how to be a front-line customer service worker.

It is key at this stage to make clear that any and all questions are welcome, even if they have been asked before. The idea is to create the safest possible environment for learning.

**Live-action learning** (Real-time decision making)

Don't keep your new hires in a classroom for long. Get them into action to learn by doing. I remember the first time I took customer service calls at Zappos. I felt so much pride — it was like we were all working together on the first NASA rocket launch.

Even though everyone was nervous, we all had support. As you take your new hires into a live environment, think about ways that they can get coaching and mentoring at a moment's notice. How can they signal to you that they need help? When we needed support on our calls at Zappos, we waved a small flag.

**Offer to turn back** (Opt-in)

During the training process, some people will realize that the job or the environment is not really a good fit for them. But the problem is that many stick with a job because they feel have to. They need the paycheck to make the rent. Therefore, it's not truly opt-in unless they feel they have total choice over the matter. That is why it's a good idea to offer them money to quit.

What's interesting is what this offer does for those who do not take it. Each person has to seriously consider if the job is worth it. By not taking the money, they are essentially investing it into their own career at the company. For those that do take the money: You've just paid a very small insurance fee for what could have been disaster.

**Challenges** (Quests)

Issue challenges throughout the training. Test them on their knowledge. Give them projects they can only accomplish by working together, and add consequences. At Zappos, after a series of practice tests (smaller quests), if you do not get 90 percent or higher on the final exam, then you are let go.

**The Oath**

Once they are finally accepted, consider how each new hire will seriously uphold the core values. The values serve as "the law," and it's up to each employee to maintain them. One way to do this is to have them swear an oath. Even though you can do it in a fun and playful manner, swearing an oath internalizes a true feeling of the importance and seriousness the values deserve.

### Celebrate!

Don't forget to celebrate their accomplishment! They have just graduated. Have people throughout the company come to cheer them, and end it with some kind of food and drink to mark this moment in their lives.

This is the full process of induction, described as a game. Here's a simple breakdown with Zappos as the example:

In its most basic format, the Zappos on-boarding process is a game:

- Goal: Get into Zappos. (Even though you've been hired, it's not guaranteed.)
- Rules: Arrive at 7am every day for four weeks. 90 percent or above required on the final test.
- Feedback: Coaching, practice quizzes.
- Opt-in: A month's salary offer to quit.

Remember, you can always start simple just by trying a few of these out.

# ● Team Initiation

We covered the process of on-boarding someone into the company, but what about inducting a new hire to your team? It is very possible that certain people will immediately take to a team's subculture, but others could have a hard time. Instead of having a new hire struggle by constantly having to figure things out by trial and error, why not set people up for success?

Here are a few introductory activities that will make the transition easier:

### 1. Introduction letter
Creating a welcome letter providing tips and tricks can start your newbie off right. At Zappos Insights, we thought it was important to introduce our unique boisterous group of passionate people and provide our new team member with some context for our group. Below is the letter we would send a few days before they joined the team. (Versions of the letter would continue to evolve over time, but here is a start to give you an idea.)

---

### Welcome to Zappos Insights!

You are about to enter one of the most exciting, unique experiences you may ever have.

Zappos Insights hosts people who are interested in learning all of Zappos's best practices and what has launched us into the #6 best place to work. Sometimes our guests are excited, others are reserved, and some are skeptical as to how Zappos capitalizes on fun and happiness in the working world.

ZI is a fast-paced environment. Anything and everything can happen. You will be expected to jump, ready to do whatever needs to be done to make things happen. This sometimes includes long hours, unconventional or unexpected tours, or unloading 3,000 copies of *Delivering Happiness* off a truck in under an hour.

---

We have many happy hours, social events, and crazy get-togethers. With that, we have many people who want to test our service. Sometimes you can feel backed into a corner or taken advantage of. The key thing to remember is that our job is to out-wow expectations. That's why we are here, and that's why thousands of people are visiting to learn.

My advice to you:

- Music appreciation is your friend. You will need to tolerate a wide range of musical tastes. Often simultaneously.
- Learn to dodge. Finger rockets are everywhere. Seriously.
- Learn all you can, ask questions, volunteer for everything. Seeing how things work is the best way to gain perspective.
- Take a deep, cleansing breath. Being able to separate yourself from the chaos will be key. If you let it build up, you will freak out.

Most importantly, this team wants you to succeed. We chose you for your skills, talents, and wonderful ability to convey the Zappos Family to our guests from around the world. Please ask us for help, encouragement, and support. That's what we are here for.

Welcome aboard!

### 2. Team shadowing

Having a new person sit with other people on the team as they do their job is a great way for the newbie to learn about how the entire team operates as well as each individual's job responsibilities. This is not a time to chitchat; it's a time for them to really observe, ask questions, and maybe even try a few new tasks on their own. Even though this may have nothing to do with their own job, it builds understanding and could provide a good framework for understanding how their job relates to the big picture.

### 3. Big brother / Big sister

Establishing a mentoring relationship within the group is a great way to foster open communication. Ideally, the mentor will go out to lunch with the newbie a few times during their first month. The mentor can also see how the new hire is interacting with the team and give feedback that other team members might not feel comfortable giving.

## ● New Manager Introduction

When a new manager is introduced to a team (or a new hire or team member is introduced to their new manager), there are a lot of unknown variables. If they are not addressed explicitly, there is a chance that there will be many bumps and hiccups as people get to know each other (especially if they are or were friends and now have a new dynamic to their relationship).

At the team level, it's best for the new manager to announce that he or she will spend most of their time listening and learning about the team and their processes for a while before making big changes. When appropriate, the first changes usually should involve clearing out a roadblock that frustrates the team as a whole. This conveys that the new manager is attentively listening and builds faith with the rest of the team.

As for the one-on-one relationships, following is a template for a manager to use for that first private discussion. Notice the meta-structure where the team member speaks first by answering the question. As a manager you are in an authority position, so anything you say will influence their answer. Thus, it's best to hear them out first, although you have the final say.

- ✔ What makes for a great boss?
- ✔ How do you like to be managed?
- ✔ How I like to manage…
- ✔ What are your expectations of me?
- ✔ Here are my expectations of you…
- ✔ What would make you feel comfortable and safe here?
- ✔ What are your goals? How would you like to grow?
- ✔ Here is the growth plan I see for you…
- ✔ Here are the decisions I trust you to make…
- ✔ Here are the decisions I would like you to run by me…
- ✔ How will I know you're doing well? (enjoying, learning, performing)
- ✔ Here is the information I will need from you (data, stats, updates, etc.)…
- ✔ Here is a guideline about how I'd like you to communicate with me… (what medium, how often, what level of detail)
- ✔ If you disagree with me, here is how I would like you to handle it… (e.g. privately)

Once this is complete, write up a summary of the meeting, and have them look it over so that you are very clear on your agreement. (Remember, clear goals and rules are needed for a good game.)

Have each party sign it. Ideally, all will be smooth sailing on the level of their commitment because you've taken the time to do this, and have both signed it (as if it were a legal document, which conveys gravity). In a worst case, you have tangible proof that someone committed to a set of behaviors and did not perform, and thus you have grounds for termination.

## ○ SERVE AND DELIVER

Now that people have been properly brought into your culture, it's time to get to work! The word execution is what comes to mind for most people, but it's still part of that older military analogy. (It means "to kill.")

With customers and clients, *it's about serving needs and delivering on promises.* It's time to focus on the delivery of value, to everyone — that means to the customer and client, to co-workers, to bosses, to vendors, to partners.

If you're in start-up mode, then your focus will be on the customer because you are rushing to get the business model sustainable before you run out of cash. But once you have reliable, regular monthly income coming in, then it's time to recognize all stakeholders with whom you have agreements.

Articulating these value propositions will make it much easier. Here we'll talk about how to create the service mindset, build up skills, and hold people accountable.

## ● World Class Service

Serving and delivering is all about *how* you do what you do. The products change and services change. Even business models change. But how you treat customers should not, and if done correctly, it could be what makes the most impact.

In any business venture, there is *always someone being served.* Without service there is no customer; without a customer, there is no revenue. So if you're not in the service game, you're in a losing game.

The same dynamic exists within your company. Each department is serving another. Employees serve managers, and managers serve employees. But sometimes we can lose sight of this. Sometimes we get so caught up in the day-to-day of work and delivery that we forget that it's real people whom we serve.

It's empowering to tell people that at any time they can raise a flag and ask this question:

*"In service to what?"*

This question usually clarifies what a disagreement or confusion is really about. When you ask this question, in any context, it forces people to consider what value is being expressed. And when it becomes a conversation about values, that's when people can get past the personal and find their alignment.

Asking how you can be of service is a powerful question, but remember that how you serve yourself actually comes first. *Leaders can do more to influence their culture just by the way they walk into the room than by a strategic decision.*

And if you're going to walk into a room with total confidence, you need to understand the next principle.

Zappos defines providing WOW! customer service as creating unique experiences to meet or exceed a customer's expectations (under-promise and over-deliver).

By creating unique shopping experiences, their hope is that customers will evangelize for Zappos and tell their friends and family to do business with them. Word of mouth has been one of the driving factors of a 75 percent repeat-customer rate year over year. The company strives to spread happiness by providing the best customer service and experience possible.

Unfortunately, in many companies, the customer service department is viewed as a pure "cost" and representatives are given incentives to "sell, sell, sell!" as a way to try to reduce that "cost." *In shifting the focus away from the "cost" and towards the "investment" that is being made through the customer experience, the entire attitude of the company and service departments can change.*

### Retention over growth

It costs far more to acquire a new customer than it does to keep a current customer (who can spread the word if they love your product or service). Thus it's counterproductive when companies focus on growth rather than aiming for a near-zero attrition rate.

### WOWing internal and external customers

The old adage "The customer is always right" is one that has lost meaning. While we may not agree that the customer is always right, they are always special. Let me repeat what I said earlier: *Without customers, our businesses are nothing.* Customers are precisely what allow a business to survive.

When we are talking about customers, we are not only referring to external customers but *internal* customers as well — all of the various departments within an organization that you work with on a daily basis.

It is easy to forget that the external success of an organization is positively correlated to its internal success. How often do you take the time to make someone within your organization feel special? What do you think would happen if you did?

When your internal customer is happy and made to feel special, your external customer will feel this as well. When internal customers are supported and made to feel special, conversations flow more smoothly, teams work more cohesively, and communication and trust increases. When your internal customers are acknowledged and celebrated, it is only a matter of time before the external customers feel the same. Having internal customers means that you treat any interaction in the same way that you would treat it with an external customer.

> *How do your team members interact with each other? Are they of service? How does your company take care of your internal customers (employees)? What improvements would positively affect your employees?*

Here are a few ways that you can drive service into the culture of the organization:

1. Have leaders embody service by taking on front-level roles from time to time.
2. Empower your people to make decisions on their own, and accept that they may fail, as long as they're learning.
3. Don't measure call times or use scripts (more on that in the next section).
4. Make it easy for people to contact you.
5. Celebrate stories of success.

Perhaps most importantly: *Hire people who value service.* If you get people who value service, then you're only training them "how" rather than fighting their behaviors.

# ● The New Service Model

The past model for service (especially phone-based customer service) has been using scripts. It's a command and control model that worked when the results were a whole lot more predictable. But technology has increased the rate of change so quickly that we need a different framework to address the unexpected.

When chaos appears, when the choice is unclear, and when there must be a response immediately, here is a new model to guide behavior:

### Stories

On the left, we have stories. Stories are examples to model. They are essentially micro case studies of what has happened before that give one a moral compass and a reference for future similar scenarios. For example, there are stories of what occurred when a customer called into Zappos in a panic two days before their wedding. It's easy to remember the narrative, and then forget about it — until the time comes up when a rep has to deal with that same situation.

So the question is: *What mechanisms do you have for capturing and sharing stories within your organization?*

### Tools

On the right we have tools. This is a team member's arsenal for delivering great service. At Zappos, call reps have over one hundred of them. This goes beyond technology and even beyond coupons and discounts. Tools can include techniques like using a customer's name on the call, and also getting them to laugh.

Here are examples of more tools:

• Make sure to check other websites when the company does not have what the customer wants.

• Never rush the phone call — reassure customer that you

have all the time in the world. Search other sites for additional product information.

- Provide a warm transfer — there should be no need for a customer to repeat information.
- Adjust your tone and speed to match the customer's.
- Find personal points of connection to talk about.
- Send personalized "thank-you" cards.
- Walk a customer through the process rather than just sending instructions.
- Instead of "How may I help you?" try "How may I serve you?"
- Make the customer laugh!

### The power of slogans and acronyms

You can encapsulate your service philosophy in a phrase or acronym that clearly describes your procedure. Starbucks uses LATTE. It's simple, but each step is critical and reduces anxiety for any employee dealing with an irate customer.

**L** isten completely to the customer.

**A** cknowledge the problem.

**T** ake action to resolve the problem.

**T** hank the customer for bringing the situation to your attention.

**E** ncourage the customer to return.

## ● Use Data Collectors

How can we actually verify that we are serving our customers well?

The only way to know what people really want and need is to ask them. Simple questions such as "What frustrates you?" and

"What do you want to change?" are great places to start. The easiest way to do that is just by sending out a simple survey. You may be surprised by what you hear.

The best way to tell if something is working well is by using a very simple tool called the Net Promoter Score (NPS). It's the feedback method of choice for companies like Apple, Amazon, Zappos and many others.

The idea behind it is that we will tolerate a poor experience for ourselves, but we would not put our name to it when recommending it to others. Therefore customer satisfaction surveys are not as accurate as a customer promoter survey.

Thus the "Ultimate Question" (as articulated in the book *The Ultimate Question* by Fred Reichheld) is:

*"How likely are you, on a scale from 0-10, to recommend this _____ to a friend or colleague?"*

The scoring mechanism is then weighted so that it recognizes that people who think negatively of an experience (detractors) are far more likely to speak out than people who had a positive experience (promoters).

Here is the scoring mechanism:
(The score ranges 200 points, from −100% to +100%)

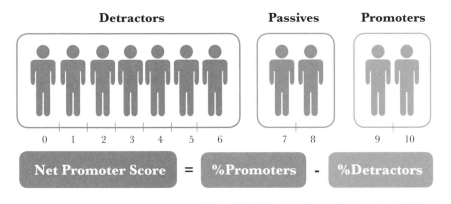

So for example, if you have 10 responses with 2 promoters, 6 detractors and 2 passives, this calculates to 20% - 60%, so your Net Promoter score would be –40%.

You can use this mechanism for scoring customer promotion, but you can also use it for your internal service testing by asking:

*How likely are you to recommend your team?*
*How likely are you to recommend your manager?*
*How likely are you to recommend this class?*
*How likely are you to recommend working at this company?*

### How to focus on metrics

Most companies place the responsibility of metrics on individuals, but feel that the culture is a group responsibility. In my experience, this does not work. It puts too much pressure for people to control what they can't (company performance) and it let's them assume others are taking care of the culture. Instead, try this:

*Performance metrics are a group responsibility: We take it on as a team. Culture is an individual responsibility: We each are fully responsible.*

# ○ ENGAGE AND SUSTAIN

Okay, now we can finally start talking about engagement. Do you see why it would be premature to do so before this point? Engagement is fascinating. While it's still a military term in one sense, it also has a certain controversy to it that's ripe for discussion. You'll see why in this section. Sustaining is all about keeping that service engine going, even through the most boring of tasks.

An engaged workforce is the golden ticket — driven employees who are passionate, active, constantly innovating, taking it to the next level, and owning projects as if the business was theirs. So the question is: What drives engagement?

At a basic level, the answers include:

### Appropriate pay and outstanding benefits

Pay does not have to be high, but it does have to meet a base standard of living. Even more important are benefits like health insurance. When people associate the health and safety of their families with their employer, they stick around. I recommend investing as much as you can, so that they pay as little out-of-pocket as possible. It's a big driver for people to stay with your company.

### Opportunities to excel

Everyone wants to grow and to progress. This does not necessarily mean position changes. It can also mean education and interesting projects. The next section, "Dynamic Learning," covers this in detail.

### Clear feedback

One of the greatest frustrations an employee can have is not knowing where he or she stands. This uncertainty can be completely unsettling, even for your strong performers. Regular feedback is key, especially feedback at the moment when work is being completed. For excellent techniques on this, read *The One Minute Manager* by Ken Blanchard.

# ● Personalized Engagement

The truth is each individual is motivated differently. Here is a framework for a manager to understand what engages different members of the team. Most people prefer a combination of several motivators. A conversation asking about their favorite moments in work will reveal one or more of the following:

### Autonomy

This is the desire to have a say in the direction of their work, to chart their own course. It's the desire to have authority over their domain, without being micromanaged.

### Mastery

This is the desire to take what they already do well and become completely proficient at it. The expert level is when they can do it with excellence on their own. The mastery level is when they can not only do it, but also teach it to others.

### Purpose

This is the desire to be part of something bigger or to work on something with meaning. Having a higher level of purpose beyond the day-to-day work can drive people to stay focused and work harder.

### Skill building

This is the desire to learn new skills, beyond one's current role.

### Accomplishments

This is the desire to achieve goals. Those who have this desire are not happy with routine work. They need projects that can be completed so they can then move on to the next one.

### Affiliation

The desire for affiliation is to work with people whom one respects, admires and learns. These people are motivated by the opportunity to work with others, perhaps across departments or even collaborating with people in other companies.

# ● Coach Up or Coach Out

When things are going askew with a team member, it's an opportunity to "Coach up, or coach out." This is a great way to come from caring about your people and wanting the best for them. If he or she made it through both the attraction and initiation process, odds are that that person is a good fit, and it's likely that something has changed.

The coaching process involves simply taking him or her aside and asking what's going on. Has something changed? Is there something in their personal lives that's affecting their work? Is there something we don't know about that is happening at work? Go into the conversation with curiosity.

Once you discuss the reason for the change, look to see if they are honest and accountable. Do they take full responsibility for the change or slip? Or do they blame others and/or blame circumstance as if it's not their fault? If they take responsibility, look to assess their level of commitment to move forward. If they are not sure about it, have a conversation about whether the company is still the right place for them. Maybe they would be happier elsewhere, and if that's the case, encourage them to think along these lines.

If they feel that the company is still the right place for them, then follow this action:

1. Make sure they are in agreement (in no uncertain terms) about what you need from them to do their job and fit with the culture.
2. Co-create an action that they will take immediately to get them

going in the right direction. It could be a small project. Their willingness to do this will show how open they are to changing. And their follow-through will show if they are accountable. Make sure you both agree on the due date, and that it is a reasonable amount of time.

3. Write this all up via email and send it to them, asking them to confirm their understanding. When there is no paper trail, then it's hard for everyone to recall what was said.

4. Check on them during the process. Ask if they need help, feedback, etc. If they are not open to help and they also do not fulfill their promise, then this is a clear sign that it's time to let them go.

**Time to fire**

When this process does not work out, or if there was an unforgivable mistake that violated the company's values or an action that would ultimately hurt your culture if you allowed this person to stay, it's time to fire. Whatever the reason, this situation can be very emotional; however, you must not waver on your commitment or someone could take advantage of your doubt.

Make sure to check with a Human Resources professional about what you must say and what you must not say. If you don't carry this process out according to law, then the company can find itself in a lawsuit.

Once you do it, make sure to talk to your team immediately. To protect the privacy of the person, keep it vague, but relate it back to the core value that was not adhered to, or the job duty that was not fulfilled. Let them share their feelings and ask questions about anything that may be on their minds. Reinforce the idea that they never have to wonder if they are not doing a good job; anyone who is not fulfilling the values or their agreed duties should be fully aware of this. It would be unfair to keep them in the dark.

### Freedom to voice ideas

People want to feel heard, even if their ideas are not used. You'll need a systematic way to take in feedback, ideally through multiple channels (examples include online services that crowdsource and prioritize ideas, regular meetings with management, a dedicated email address, such as ideas@yourcompany.com, and quarterly surveys).

# ● Dynamic Learning

Beyond the basics, however, the best way to keep people engaged is to ensure they are growing through learning. But not all learning is equal. Here are the techniques to keep learning active, alive and engaging.

### Didactic learning

This simply means telling someone what they will learn (as a benefit) and then explaining it to them. So rather than just giving information, first explain the context and the value of the information, and then provide it. Finally, sum it up at the end as "key takeaways."

### Stories and case studies

Stories are a great way to convey information and stimulate conversation, especially when people have fun with them.

### Experiential learning

Having a live experience (especially using more than one sense) allows one to learn through new feelings and gain new perspectives. For example this can include games, scavenger hunts, parades, skits, etc.

### Reflection

New information or experiences can quickly be forgotten. It's important to create time for reflection in the form of silence, thinking, and writing to give people the opportunity to let the lessons sink in and understand how they affect them.

### Sharing

Whether in a big group, dyads, or triads, sharing insights and experiences gives people the chance to verbalize and articulate what they've learned. It becomes easier to remember, and also impacts other people around them.

### Exercises

Ask questions to get people thinking, such as how to apply a certain lesson to their jobs. This makes the information relevant and gets them to consider actions and practices.

### Hot seats

Have someone come up and share their story, with the facilitator and audience coaching them through their situation. The group first offers questions to help them think about their situation, then offers solutions.

### Learning by doing

This is trial by fire. Simply doing what one has just learned as information is the fastest, deepest way to know it. It's high-risk and high-reward.

### Gain commitment and accountability

There is a lot of energy after a great class, so it's important to leverage it right then and there. This is the time to ask people to publicly share their goals and commitments. It's also time to ask them how they will keep themselves accountable.

# ● Unbreakable Rituals

If you think about it, most of your life is made up of habits. Go through your day and much of it is routine — some are healthy routines, others are not so healthy. Rituals are habits on a group level. Companies that proactively design their rituals create strong cultures.

**Remember to celebrate.**

When I was at Zappos, many types of businesses came through every year. And the interesting trend I noticed was that no matter how big or small, how successful or how struggling, they all seemed to forget where they came from and how far they'd come. The truth is that if you're in business at all, you're doing something right because people are finding value in your service. Thus there is always something to celebrate, and this is the big difference between success and *fulfillment.*

Think about growing up as a kid and going to school, from elementary school to junior high to high school. Can you imagine what it would have been like it you hadn't had a weekend at the end of every school week? Imagine if the schooldays just kept on going, and you had to wake up early every day and go to class. Can you imagine what a beaten-down zombie you would feel like after a while? Weekends were absolutely necessary and invigorating. They were a predictable break where we could relax with our friends and family. We had our snack times, favorite sports, TV and games. Remember how they made the whole school week worthwhile?

As grown-ups, although our weekends sometimes get frazzled, our lives are still filled with other, similar "unbreakable rituals." These are also necessary, invigorating and predictable events that happen no matter how good or bad things are going. We come to rely on them; they are like a return home.

We actually have the power to do this within organizations. But very few do.

The unbreakable rituals of a business can vary from a fifteen-minute morning power-up meeting to an all-company meeting (To this day, the founders of Google still hold Friday town-hall meetings).

Another example is a monthly team-building event. Usually organizations think to do this only when things are going badly, and the team needs to come together. But why not keep that from ever happening? A monthly team-building event outside the office does not have to be fancy. In fact, going hiking at a local park is completely free. The idea is to schedule unstructured time with team members in a new environment, so that you build that team and family spirit.

Here are ways (from the simple to the extravagant) that you can build in celebration (ideally, as an unbreakable ritual).

### Morning meeting

This is a simple format that can change your mornings (it's also mentioned in the "Troubleshooting" section).

### 1. A gratitude, win or excitement

Simply have each person on the team say one thing that he or she is grateful for, or mention some kind of win. So often, we achieve something, but no one else sees it! This is a way to share it in a healthy way such that the whole team can celebrate it.

### 2. Focus

Have each person share his or her focus for the day. This way everyone hears what the one big achievement would be for everyone that day.

### 3. The break

Finally end with a chant, for example the "Ready…break!" of a football huddle. **Note:** This type of meeting seems to work for teams of twenty or less, and can be done in less than fifteen minutes.

### All-hands meeting

Take time to stop and come together as a company to celebrate what you've achieved, and what you're planning for the future. Google actually does this with their founders once a week.

Perhaps the most daring example at Zappos is the all-hands meeting. It's a five-hour event, held quarterly, where they shut down the entire call center and over one thousand employees gather in a theater. It's filled with announcements, updates, songs, dance numbers, guest speakers, and videos, all ending with a big celebration.

It makes no sense for their bottom line. It makes no sense not to take calls from customers, but it's a rich tradition that unifies the company in a way that is simply amazing.

Here is the format for an actual all-hands meeting at Zappos:

- Pre-show opening number (sheer entertainment and fun)
- Go over last quarter's financials
- Live Q&A with CEO (on the fly transparency)
- KaBOOM! Speaker (all about how important play is)
- Past video bloopers (fun)
- Skill share (a presentation on a new way for everyone to teach each other)
- Sir Ken Robinson (TED speaker on creativity)
- Corporate Challenge winner announcement (sports competition with other companies in Las Vegas)
- Z-Endurance (a program that pays employees the entrance fee to any sports competition they enter)

- Fashion show (new products on the web site)
- College interns (video introducing new interns)
- Charity update (about how helping the local and worldwide community)
- Innovation Experience (a new program giving randomly drawn employees a bonus to spend on an innovation project)
- Zappendales (an hysterical Zappos boy-band video)
- Happy hour! (an outdoor picnic of drinks, food and a band)

# ● Schedule the Celebrations

So what can you start scheduling immediately?

Even if your company is virtual, you can do a standing weekly (or even daily) phone call to get everyone up to speed and powered up. The point is this: Can you make your own company so important that no matter what, the unbreakable ritual is not cancelled? That's how you build lasting strength. That (in combination with supporting constant growth and learning) is how you can keep most of your people for a lifetime.

**Schedule your celebrations.**
Celebrations are usually an afterthought... *"We did really well this year — we should throw some kind of party or something."* But sometimes even that doesn't happen! Instead, schedule them in advance. Assume victory, because if you are in any kind of business today, that means you are providing amazing value that people are willing to pay for.

Here is how you convert a regular happy hour into a celebration: First, don't have it after work. People have families. They want to go home, and they want to recharge for you so that they can be strong the next day. Make it on the early side, ideally 4pm, but no later than 5:30pm. Next, plan it as a celebration. What can you announce? What games can you play? What video could you show? In other words, what will make this *memorable?*

# ● Policy Design: The 99% Rule

Every organization has policies. In a word, they're rules. They say what's okay and what's not okay. Unfortunately, many organizations fall into the trap of ever-expanding rules built upon rules that begin to look like the country's tax code. When that happens, at best people tune them out as much as possible. At worst (like the tax code), they actively figure out ways to get around them. Sometimes this is necessary to simply get their job done, or take care of a customer.

Instead, consider the idea that *less is more.*

The best visual designers know that it's not about what you add to a piece of work as much as it is about what you can take away. Take the iPod. There were many other mp3 players at the time of its development, but the simplicity of the design was what made it so elegant — not a lot of features and buttons.

Unfortunately, most policy design is not really about design at all. It's about ramming in every potential scenario. And even though the intentions are good, the outcome is bad, because it's simply ineffective.

Let's use the example of a dress code. In corporate America, there are all kinds of different guidelines on what is appropriate and not appropriate to wear. And as fashion changes, this leads to more policy changes and more meetings. I have heard of companies that have spent hours discussing what a "flip-flop" sandal is and what constitutes an appropriate versus inappropriate flip-flop. Seriously.

Meanwhile, this is the dress code policy at Zappos: *Don't offend anyone.*

Yes, it's that simple. How does it work? Well, let's say someone wears something offensive. It is then some other employee's responsibility to be an adult and either inform the offender in a private conversation, or let that person's manager know. And then it's resolved in discussion (which is easy when everyone is aligned in their values. Otherwise it's a longer conversation). So rather than using the entire company's time, we've isolated it to those who have a problem with it.

*"Less is more" means planning for and supporting the 99 percent who are "good," rather than defending against the 1 percent who break a policy.*

A similar, flexible approach applies to policies towards customers. Most companies are very stringent in enforcing their policies, but if they took a look at the data, it is usually less than 5 percent of their customers who actually abuse a policy. And yet the amount of time and energy focused on that 5 percent is much more than 5 percent of the company's time. What makes it even worse is that the data show that customers who have a negative experience are five times more likely to proactively speak badly about a company than those who have a great experience. In other words, your policy breakers are a huge liability! If they don't like how they were treated, it doesn't even matter if they were wrong! They are going out of their way to try to make sure you do not succeed.

Yes, you are right that they have broken your policy, but their percentage is trivial. Would you rather stay right and be upset with them, only to have them go speak badly about your brand? Or would you rather give up being right and stay happy while making your customers happy?

One way to resolve this is through a "one-time exception" rule. Allow them the transgression, but let them know that it is a break in a policy to which they agreed, and that it will only be this one time. If the customer repeatedly takes advantage of this, then inform them that you do not seem to be meeting their needs and "invite" them to shop elsewhere.

If you still are resistant to this idea that less is more, consider what it is like to be a parent. It's one thing if you have a couple of kids, but imagine having fifteen of them. How would you do it? "Don't have too many rules" — that is what parents with a lot of kids say. One even said, "We only have two rules: You must be safe, and you must be polite." Every possible transgression fit into one of those categories.

When you have few rules, then you empower people to make decisions for themselves, rather than micromanaging.

## ● Empowerment

Micromanaging was actually a good strategy for an industrial-based economy and mass production. Business is completely different today. There are so many decisions to make on a moment-to-moment basis that you simply cannot define or predict the best actions. Instead, if we can use the right guidelines and parameters, people will know what to do. And if they are truly empowered, they will not be scared to make mistakes.

Most importantly, to keep your employees with your company for the long-term, remember that people want to be treated like people. They don't want to feel like cogs in a machine.

At Zappos, employees are empowered to make decisions that are right for the business to serve customers. Since the core values serve as a framework for making decisions, Zappos trusts that employees will use their best judgment and do the right thing.

During the Zappos.com Las Vegas Rock and Roll Marathon back in December 2011, a family was on their way to see *The Lion King* at the Mandalay Bay Hotel. The father was taking his daughter to the show for her tenth birthday. This day was quite hectic since the city closed Las Vegas Boulevard down for the race, and car traffic was in gridlock for over two hours. Due to all the chaos with the marathon, the family missed the show.

The father was upset and he emailed Tony to express his disappointment. He reached out to Tony because Zappos sponsored the marathon. The father said that he didn't want *Lion King* tickets since his daughter had no desire to see the show anymore. What he asked for instead was the experience to have his daughter see firsthand how Zappos would handle the situation.

One of Tony's assistants, Valerie, read and responded to the email. She was on a mission to make up for what had happened and did her best to make the family happy.

Valerie worked quickly and thought of a few ideas to resolve the problem. She took charge of the situation without any management approval. The first thing she did was to invite the family to tour the office. In preparation for their visit, Valerie got balloons for the little girl and ordered a birthday cake.

When the family arrived for their tour, Valerie gave the birthday girl the balloons, and then they started to tour the office. Midway through the tour, they stopped at a desk that had a birthday cake, and the girl noticed her name on it. All of a sudden the Zapponians that were working in that area started singing "Happy Birthday". This was such an emotional experience created for this family, and the girl was elated and her father was overwhelmed.

A week later, the family sent flowers to Zappos. Valerie and the other Zapponians who worked that day who were able to turn a big disappointment around.

There are always going to be challenges that require quick thinking to solve. Many times employees can't get management approval on every single issue that arises. The solution is to empower your employees to solve problems themselves. If you've hired the right people who are aligned with your company's core values, then the values will serve as a decision-making framework. When you can instill trust in your employees that they'll do the right thing, it makes your business scalable.

## ● Epic Engagement

Any company can do what we've covered thus far. So what happens when another company comes along with all of these approaches plus a bigger brand name, higher pay, or a better city? Do you just chalk that up to the nature of the game? Or are you interested in the real differentiator — the key to driving long-term engagement that is so strong that people would accept below-average pay, or even stay in a city they don't like?

The key to long-term epic engagement is... drama.

"What? Drama?"

Yes, you heard me right. It's *drama*.

There once was a reality TV show about life coaching where the premise was that the coach would help people in impossible situations. It involved all these common words surrounding engagement: passion, caring, intensity, listening to people, clear feedback, freedom, major decisions to be made — and yet it was cancelled.

Compare that to a show like *Jersey Shore*. This involves none of what we associate with an engaged environment. In fact, the people on the show are usually terrible at their jobs. And yet people are enthralled by it; they are completely engaged with the content.

Why is there such a big difference? It's because in the first show, we all know what's going to happen! The person on the show will be in a horrible situation, they'll think there's no way out, and then they will get themselves out of their situation in a heart-felt ending. There's no sense that the people on the show may fail and fall flat on their faces. So we check out. We don't care.

In other words, what I mean by drama is:

*The sense that anything can happen: It could be awful, or it could be amazing.*

Real engagement lies in a state of constant creative tension. That creative tension can often be seen like this:

Let's use the example of a call center to show the difference between engaged and non-engaged.

### Standard call center
- Safety = Just read our call script and you'll be fine.
- Freedom = Act on your own. But we will give you no guidance, and if you screw up, you're gone.

### Engaged call center
- Safety = Weeks of training, mentorship, coaching, and a precedent of rewarding learning even through failure.

- Freedom = No scripts, but you are given plenty of values-embedded stories from those who went before you, as well as an arsenal of tools.

Here are some principles and ways to use drama to your advantage:

### Build anticipation.

To really develop a true and healthy sense of drama, there has to be a cliffhanger, that chance that may turn into an epic win or a drastic failure, and with a probable opportunity to say, "I was there when it happened." The sense of anticipation comes from elusive yet attainable goals. On a group level, the goal needs to be so inspiring it requires no explanation. You simply love it, or you don't. For Zappos at the time of this writing, that's creating a thriving downtown in Las Vegas and creating a college campus for adults.

### Make personal glory achievable.

A culture of real engagement has everyday people who are living their dreams. They are living proof that you can come in as lowly as a janitor and rise through excellence to a career or calling of your choice. True, it won't happen for everyone. It takes hard work and perseverance. But an engaged culture shows that it is by no means impossible.

### Create a new kind of sexy.

What makes something sexy? Have you noticed it's never sex? Pornography isn't sexy, but intrigue and innuendo are. Nakedness isn't sexy, but lingerie is. That's because sexy is about alluding, it's about what's hidden, it's about the taboo, it's about secrets and desires. And the truth is, intrigue, innuendo, secrets and desires exist in an organizational setting — they exist in the form of people who want to laugh, who don't want to work all the time, who want to try crazy ideas, who are scared, and who want to connect deeply while knowing they have to maintain decorum.

The real engaged cultures ride the line here. They dance on the edge of inappropriate. They challenge the status quo without breaking the system. By pushing the line, they expose new truths where learning can occur; it is so different, and yet still safe.

**Family and drama go hand-in-hand.**
The strongest cultures feel like family because people are there rain or shine, fully dedicated, and sticking through it even when they're unhappy. And any strong family has a decent sense of drama — that tension that only becomes clear when we acknowledge the shadow, when we get real. The first big reality show was called *The Real World*, with the tag line *"When people stop being polite, and start getting real."*

Conduct codes, manuals, and call scripts all create a sense of false confidence that people can be controlled. But underlying it all is a much different conversation that most employers are afraid of. What they don't know is that this conversation contains the breakthroughs that could help them dominate an entire industry. But more importantly, those conversations contain the very essence of what makes their employees feel alive.

## ○ SHARE AND OBSERVE

This is the last and most underrated stage of the engine. Observation is a combination of analysis and reflection — in other words, getting data points we can use to make sure we are on target, and then reflecting on them to understand the lessons and plan for the future.

Sharing is critical and not understood well or at all at most companies. On a culture level, whatever you share will grow. Sharing can become an automatic habit that will reinforce integrity, build appreciation, and subtly develop a culture of giving without the need to receive quid pro quo.

Sharing is the counterintuitive secret that will give you the edge for decades. Common sense would say you should focus on your business, but success has shown us that companies that go beyond their employees and their paying customers actually last longer and have higher revenues than those who do not.

There are many ways you can share beyond paid products and services that will keep you relevant, keep attracting talent, and most importantly remind you of all the reasons you ever loved your business in the first place.

## ● Share to Keep

Once you've got it, you've got to give it.

Well, of course you don't *have* to do anything of the kind, but from what we've seen, the companies that share their beliefs, their stories, and their lessons develop so much goodwill from customers that it constantly reminds the business-owners why they started the business in the first place.

The adage goes: *What you share, you get to keep. What you hoard disappears.*

Yes, it may sound oddly spiritual in nature, but this is the secret formula for successful businesses and will continue to be in the future. They share their story — how they did it — and they continue to share what's going on inside, what's real, and what problems they are working on.

A great example is B-Reel, an interactive advertising agency that has created worldwide viral hits for its clients. (Their ad campaigns have been so good that consumers have made thank-you videos for their advertisements.) B-Reel actually posts videos of their experiments on its website. Many would say they are giving away their secrets. But instead it establishes the company as a powerhouse of innovation, and provides an opportunity for brands to recognize their new technologies and ask B-Reel if they can be used for their brand.

Another great example is the "Manifesto" shared by Balsamiq. com. They share themselves, their lives, and their methodology so freely that it's a joy to read. Even if you don't use their product!

What is it that your company stands for? How can you be a beacon for what you believe? And then how can you share it? There are so many ways: blogs, tours, or creating your own culture book to share with the world. (See an example of the Zappos culture book at www.CultureBook.org.)

I would love to hear your examples of sharing your culture. Email me at Robert@CultureBlueprint.com.

# Chapter Four

## Implementation

The key to keeping anything going is implementing a system. Would you want to have to constantly check on quality and peer in on every aspect of your business? Or would you rather have a system take care of it?

Most people are familiar with systems when it comes to production, but culture itself can be systematized. The system starts at the very beginning, at the idea stage:

*Where will you start?*
*How will you get ideas?*
*Which ideas will work best?*

*How can you test the idea?*
*How do you make sure it doesn't spark, then die out?*
*How do you build people's skills to turn ideas into reality?*

This section will answer all of these questions and more.

# ◯ IDEATION

At this point you might be swimming with ideas. Ideation is all about gathering those ideas, thinking them through, and picking one to start with.

### 1. Gather your ideas.

*What ideas have you taken thus far from the book?*
*What are ideas from other companies that you would like to try?*
*What experience do you want to have every day at your company?*
*What would be a ritual that would make that experience come to life?*

Look through the "Culture Toolkit" and "Troubleshooting" sections if you need more ideas.

It's best if you can gather your ideas in some kind of visual way. Sticky notes are ideal because you can move them around and they're visual and tangible.

### 2. Select either the idea with longest effect or highest leverage.

A long effect means it will last for generations. So, for example, that might be discovering and implementing your core values. It's not the easiest or shortest journey, but it certainly has a long effect.

High leverage means it will have a high output with low input. Zappos calls this "Do more with less." Letting someone go is an example of this. It takes no resources to let go someone who you know isn't a culture fit. But the impact is huge and it's felt the very next day. You can see more examples of this in the "Immediate Wins" section.

### 3. Write down every thought, goal, and obstacle connected to the selected idea.

Before we go into the process of turning it into reality, write down all your thoughts, emotions, hesitations, and big wins that you connect to this idea. Then write down why this idea is important to you.

# ⃝ EXPERIMENTS OVER PROTOTYPES

Have you ever tried to pitch a project or a change and found that people are resistant? Do you know why? No matter what the details, it's because they don't believe it will work. They have no way of knowing for certain, but their experiences in life have led them to believe it will not work. But the question is *not* how can you talk them out of their current belief. The question is how you can you get what you need without requiring them to change their beliefs.

**Enter the beta test.**

The beta is a test. It's an experiment. Note that it's not a pilot, it's not a program, and it's not an initiative, because all of those things come with the fear that if they don't work, then there will be a lot of damage as a result. But an experiment is a small, cheap, fast, and easy way to determine if your hypothesis is correct. It's very scientific in that sense: It either achieves its goal or it doesn't. Or perhaps it achieves a secondary, unintended goal. (The sticky note was developed out of a "failed" adhesive that did not permanently stick).

The beta test idea comes from the software world. For culture purposes, it's a way to scale back the scope of a change, such that you can learn from it. The big mistake is to put a lot of energy, time, and money into a company-wide change without even knowing how well it will work. Even a pilot will not work because there is often far too much energy and attention required to justify the risk. Instead, small experiments will quickly show you what works and what does not.

Let's go into the blueprint within the blueprint to show you how to make this happen.

# ○ THE BETA BLUEPRINT

**Know your goal.**

Once you've picked the change you want to make, it's important to be specific about what it is, and why you feel it's important.

**Determine the gatekeeper and stakeholders.**

The gatekeeper is anyone who holds the resources you need to do this (money, personnel, space, etc.). If you have a culture that already values innovation and you don't need resources, then you often don't need permission (provided that you limit the downside). The stakeholders are anyone who would ultimately be affected by what you're trying.

**Plan your pitch.**

Before approaching someone, really get in touch with your passion and excitement. It's infectious.

Next, the point is not to "sell" or get "buy-in" or to change someone's mind. The point is to offer your belief as a hypothesis, and ask for what you need such that you can test it without doing any serious damage if you're wrong. The way you figure that out is by taking any big idea you have, and shrinking its dimensions. If you are in the start-up world, this could also be considered a "pivot" within the lean methodology.

**Dimension to adjust:**
- Scope (reduction in amount of work)
- Reach (reduction in number of people it will affect)
- Duration (reduction in overall length of the test)
- Segment (change in test audience)
- Value (change in metric that will be improved)
- Cost (figure out how it can be done for less money)
- Technology (use something rudimentary, or even paper)

Let's use an example. Let's say you want to revamp your entire attraction (recruiting) process. That's a big deal, and if there's already a process there, it could be very disruptive. But we can easily find our beta test if we run it through the dimensions:

| | |
|---|---|
| **Scope** | Change from the entire recruiting process to only the interview |
| **Reach** | Use only one department |
| **Duration** | Limit the test to only one month |
| **Segment** | Switch departments or groups to one that is more open to a test |
| **Value** | Switch test to the application process because CEO cares more about attracting applicants |
| **Cost** | Reduce number of hours by limiting the number of interviews |
| **Technology** | Rather than installing a candidate tracking system, use Microsoft Excel |

You can keep playing with the dimensions until you get a green light for your beta test. **Note:** You may have to do this on the spot while you're pitching it.

### Pick a scoring mechanism.

It's tempting to assume that the beta test will either go well or it won't, but life is hardly that black and white. What is your success criterion? How will you know whether it was successful and to what degree? You have to pick how you're going to keep score in this game (Hint: pick something that your stakeholders really care about).

### Scoring Mechanisms:
- Increases (revenue, profit)
- Decreases (absenteeism, injuries, time spent)
- Experience quality (Net Promoter Score)
- Engagement Index (happiness, fulfillment, activity, contribution)

**Make it emotionally relevant.**

Joseph Stalin, the Soviet dictator, said, "One death is a tragedy. A million deaths is a statistic." When we make it personal, it all becomes real and it hits home. So let's say your goal is to reduce employee turnover. Turnover is just a statistic. But think about one powerful story, or one powerful employee. And get your audience to imagine losing that one person, then multiplying that by 100. People make decisions by emotions. So bring it back to a story and make it real.

**Practice your pitch.**

Now that you have it all mapped out, it's time to address your blind spots. If you are doing anything totally on your own, then you have blind spots. Would you rather discover them during the game or during practice?

Share your idea and your pitch with someone and ask them to consider the following:

*Did you feel moved by the idea?*
*Do you believe that if it were successful, it would prove valuable?*
*Do you think the beta test is limited such that it will not be a major distraction?*
*Do you think that the request is reasonable?*
*Do you think we are tracking the most important indicators of success?*

It actually helps if you think of this whole process as flirting. You don't have control of other people. Instead you're playing, you're dancing, and you're seeing if you really connect.

# ○ A BETA STORY

I was speaking with a friend at a company who was tasked with figuring out a way to create more innovation within a team, using the 80/20 principle. In this case, the company saw that Google gave its developers 20 percent of their time to work on whatever they wanted, knowing that great innovations come out of such unstructured time.

He worked on a report for six months, presented it to the COO, who read it and said, "We can't do this. This would disrupt our work too much." Dave was totally dismayed. He had poured his heart and soul into that research report, and he gave the COO exactly what he was asking for. And yet now his value to the company was actually being questioned.

But sometimes we don't even need to create an entire beta blueprint. Sometimes we can just have an inquisitive conversation, listening to what someone wants and using questions to parse out what they need. Imagine if the conversation went something like this:

**❝** Guy: *I heard Google does the 20 percent innovation time. How about you figure out how we can do it? Then we'll implement it here.*

Dave: *Okay, let's take a step back first. Tell me what you really want. Why should we do this? What would be the great win?*

Guy: *Well we could come up with major innovations we wouldn't even think of.*

Dave: *Okay, great. What would that breakthrough look like?*

Guy: *Um.... Some kind of industry-changing product.*

Dave: *Awesome. Is there any particular type of product or industry?*

Guy: *Well, I really want us to develop something for the hospitality industry.*

Dave: *Fantastic. How about we test this out in a way where we can learn what works, but if it doesn't work, we don't lose a lot of time and money.*

Guy: *That sounds perfect.*

Dave: *We'll need three guys in product development. Who comes to mind?*

Guy: *Um. Jon, Ed and Marty.*

Dave: *Great, I'll sit down with them and ask them when they can schedule 20 percent of their time, and they'll do it for thirty days, thinking about products for the hospitality industry. I'll check in with them and coach them once a week to help them with any blocks. We'll do it for a month and report on how it's going. I'll tell you the result and you tell me if it's worth it.*

Guy: *Wait... (writes on a piece of paper). That's 32 hours, times 3 people, that's 96 hours! It can't be this month we have way too much to do.*

Dave: *That's every month, Guy.*

Guy: *No, we really need to delay this.*

Dave: *Okay, well there's no getting around the fact that the time will have to come from somewhere, and I said thirty days because I thought ninety days would scare you. What amount of time would be reasonable to you?*

Guy: *Um, I'd say sixty hours.*

Dave: *Okay, great...*                                   **"**

The conversation would go on with Dave adjusting the dimensions / pivot of the conversation until Guy is at the edge of his comfort zone. Perhaps they would also change the problem to something smaller such that they can see traction sooner.

# ○ MARKET INTERNALLY

*"If you build it, they will come"* is the fallacy in all internal programs!

The problem is that people do not consider internal communications as a form of *marketing*. Everyone thinks that marketing is necessary only to attract customers. Why? Because customers have choices, and you have to get their attention, their time, and their money through influence. The error to is to assume that just because the company issues the paycheck that it also controls the attention, time, and passion of its people.

There are two reasons why a great program or initiative can go bad. First, anything new requires a change, and change is only accepted immediately when something bad is taken away. (For example, abolishing the dress code is a change that people instantly love because it's *taking away* rules. It frees people.) A change that adds time or complexity, no matter how good, will always be met with grunts and groans. The only way employees push through that is when they believe in it.

Second, there often is no buildup, no anticipation, no perceived future set of events that makes a coming change more and more intriguing. This is why Apple spends so much time focusing on their product launches. Why would they do that when people already LOVE their products? Why do existing Apple customers wait with bated breath? It's because they know that the company will create an experience, a moment in time that will later become legend, one they want to experience.

How much would you like changes at your company to feel like that?

If you're ready to start thinking about this as "internal market adoption," please eliminate the following expression from your vocabulary: *"How do we make people do _____ ?"* Why? Because you can't make anyone do anything. It all comes down to personal choice. A better question is: *"How do we find out their needs and serve them?"* The answer to this question is the core of the value proposition in your marketing roll out.

## Example: Rolling out coaching

> *"A designer is someone who changes need into demand."*
>
> — **Tom Peters** in Design.

In 2010, Zappos Insights started the Goals program as a way to systematically provide life coaching to Zappos employees. The idea behind it was that if people are achieving both their professional and personal goals as a result of a benefit offered at the company, then why would they ever leave? And if employees are struggling with issues that are troubling them, then it takes away from their concentration at work. So why not offer a great resource?

The challenge was to roll out the program in a way that would greatly benefit the company and the employees, while educating many new people about its benefits. But there was also a trap to avoid.

In researching coaching programs at other companies, I found that despite being highly effective (One top professional services firm actually calculated that coaching yielded a strong return on investment for the company), programs were often cut when times were bad because they were an easy, non-essential line item to ax. So how could the program be developed in a way that not only made it effective, but would also make people regard it as a rich tradition to be proud of and maintained?

We did a round of interviews, picked our coach (Augusta Scott), sent her to coaching school (Coaches Training Institute), and began strategizing the internal marketing rollout. Here are the steps:

### 1. Stack the deck in your favor.

You always want to start with a win. So make sure you get one. How? By starting with a small group of enthusiastic people who have opted-in. These are your champions, your super-fans. They see the benefit, and they want to go for it.

For the coaching program, we asked people to apply to be the first, and we only selected the ten most passionate. The result? A hundred percent of them achieved their goal. The program looked pretty darn effective and we could leverage that momentum to the next stage.

### 2. Don't make it available to everyone.

Rather than making coaching immediately available to everyone, we made it available gradually to more and more people. This was important not only to drive demand, it was also important for coach Augusta not to take on too much at once. Otherwise she would have become overwhelmed and done a disservice to her clients. A slower rollout builds in room for learning.

### 3. Gain small commitments.

If people make a small commitment, they are much more likely to see the whole thing through. So, for example, charities have found that it's much easier to raise money from potential donors if the prospective givers are asked to take some kind of small action first. Someone who is asked to wear a pink bow for cancer awareness (costing the wearer virtually no money) is much more likely to contribute to the cause when asked later than someone who was directly asked for money without being asked to wear the bow first.

We applied the idea of small commitments by requiring interested employees to first attend a class to learn how coaching works. (This also saved Augusta a lot of time by educating a group all at once rather than in individual sessions.) The participants then had to fill out a sheet articulating their goals in order to be scheduled for their appointment. This built clarity and commitment before the sessions even began. Lastly, it served as a way to slow down the process so that there was not a huge wave of clients all at once.

### 4. Celebrate the achievers.

Those who achieve their goal through the program are given a bracelet, a T-shirt and a pin to commemorate their win. They are also given a goals-celebration lunch where they and their peers who have achieved goals gather and celebrate together.

### 5. Socialize the success.

To make sure that people know the program is working (and to further the celebration), the achievers are announced in the middle of the call center floor where everyone can see them. They also have the opportunity to write their goal and their name on the stairway wall, and we also made a music video to share with the company.

# ○ THE CULTURE CELL

If you take a look at cultures that are working well, you'll see that unbreakable rituals and celebrations work according to the idea of the **culture cell.**

The culture cell is the most basic element of system design, applied to organizational behavior. I call it the "self-reinforcing positive feedback loop."

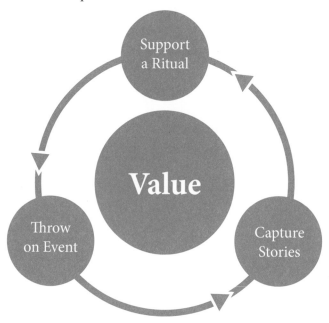

How it works is very, very simple. Let's say you value growth and learning. You then create a ritual that will make this value come to life. So let's say you have no money to spend on this and you make it a monthly lunch-and-learn. Every first Friday at lunch people gather in one area, and one team member teaches a new skill to the group.

You do the first one yourself, teaching everyone your ninja email skills that tame your inbox to zero. After that, you collect stories about how it went. Some people loved it and their lives are so much better now that they have mastered email. However, others are struggling. So how do you resolve this?

The people who have mastered it can teach the others! You then share all the success with the team (otherwise they may not even know about it), which builds excitement for the next lunch-and-learn. Next, add more structure to the ritual, or maybe add a signup sheet by person and topic, so that you can schedule them in advance.

The model grows in complexity, but only as it needs to. For example, your company may get huge and then you need a process to screen for topics so that they will be of interest to everyone, or maybe you break them up into smaller groups. Or maybe you need more structure to both capture and share success stories.

Let's get into those mechanisms...

# ○ STORY CAPTURE

Stories are all we are ever left with. They hydrate the culture as well as convey the experiences that shaped the organization. Stories become the new mythology passed on to each generation (as well as to new customers and to journalists). Today the power of video has made it easy for anyone to tell stories without even knowing how to write.

So make sure to capture the story of your first beta project.

Here are a few simple ways you can start capturing and sharing stories:

### On the spot
For less than $200, an iPod touch has the camera, microphone, and editing equipment right on board to create short films. Anyone can do it, though it's even better if you can dedicate an enthusiastic team member to the process.

### Contests
Competition always motivates. Think of fun rewards for the best customer stories.

### Stories at meetings
Consider starting meetings out with a story. Ask people to come to a meeting with a great customer story, or a challenge they overcame.

### Company history
The story of the how the company started is always very powerful. But how will it be remembered? Create a project to use various media (photos, videos, interviews, etc.) to tell the entertaining story of how the organization was founded.

Next think about where and when the story is re-told — for example, the company website, blogs, first day of work for new employees, at the company party, etc.

# ○ REINVENTION

So you've thought of an idea, you've experimented, pivoted, and succeeded. Then you captured the story. What's next? Well, the next idea, of course.

Oftentimes your next idea comes out of crisis — a change in the market, a competitor who pulls ahead, a change in technology. But the smartest companies are the ones that anticipate great changes. They don't do this by predicting the future. They do it by creating the future.

As Steve Jobs said when he announced a new iPod: "The iPod is the best-selling personal music device in the world... which is why we're completely changing it." The best way to predict the future is to create it.

Here are the questions you need to ask yourself before you start shaking things up:

1. *Do you have importance?* (Why must we do something?)
2. *Do you have urgency?* (Why must we do something NOW?)
3. *What is the immediate action/win?* (See "Immediate Wins" section, and "Culture Toolkit" in general, for ideas)
4. *Do you have regular meetings set up?* (How are we keeping this top of mind, rather than letting it slip?)
5. *Is this a "Hell, yeah!"?* (If not, ask what would make it one)

## ○ THE PROCESS OF TRANSFORMATION

In a way, it really doesn't matter where you start. What's most important is that you simply start. The experience itself will give you the wisdom and confidence to make deeper and bigger changes that will be unique to you and your organization.

Here is how that process works:

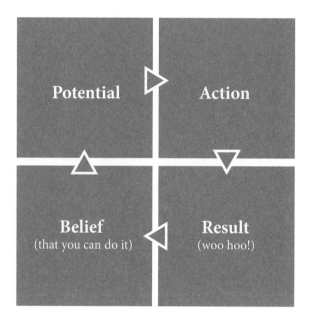

### Stage 1 - Potential
This is where the idea starts. You see an opportunity for improvement. Something frustrates you and you want to make a change. But it only stays in your mind unless you advance to Stage 2.

### Stage 2 - Action
You take some sort of action (illustrated in detail through the "Beta Blueprint"). With enough shifting and pivoting through the process you get to...

## Stage 3 - Result

You've achieved something.

## Stage 4 - Belief

Through working that muscle of achievement, you advance your belief in yourself and your own capabilities. (You've already done this your whole life.) Now, with this new belief, you take a look at new opportunities, and the cycle repeats.

So as you can see, the game we are playing is simply constantly upgrading your beliefs about what is possible, and giving you the tools to make it happen. It's a virtuous cycle that if turned into a habit becomes a self-reinforcing positive feedback loop.

### Limiting beliefs

Are you ready to start building? Are you sure? As we said, any limiting beliefs need to be noted and accounted for. For example, let's take the limiting belief *"This culture shift is going to be really hard, very time-consuming, and probably expensive."*

Do you have any beliefs like this? If so, make sure to write them down, and ask yourself:

1. Are these beliefs true?
2. I mean it. Really ask yourself: if you had to bet your life, would you be certain beyond a shadow of a doubt that this belief is true?
3. When you hold this belief, what's the cost? How do you feel? How does it affect your outlook about the future?
4. If you were to give up this belief and let it go, what opens up? What becomes possible?

(Process sourced from Byron Katie's *The Work*.)

Really think about these questions. If you do, you'll clear out your own roadblocks. And whether you do or do not, make sure to watch *The Parking Lot Movie*. (It's on Netflix). It shows how a simple parking lot was able to create a stronger culture than most corporations, with no resources.

# Chapter Five

## The Culture Toolkit

## ○ IMMEDIATE WINS

Now that you're ready for a shift, you'll want to take swift action that shows that you're serious and that more change is coming. Now, here's the beauty of it. It won't cost you anything and you will see change immediately.

I know what you're thinking. "Why didn't you just tell me this from the beginning?" It's because you weren't ready to hear it. And even if you were, there's a danger that you would get a small win and then stop there. I want you to commit to the whole plan because that will build a culture that runs well without you even needing to be there.

Over the years I have worked with hundreds of companies to determine what makes an impact in a small amount of time. Here's the magic:

### The "Reverse Beta"

Everyone knows about the "beta test" — try something new and see how it goes. (For a more prescriptive process, see the "Beta Blueprint" chapter.)

But even easier is the "Reverse Beta." This is the exact opposite. Try stopping something that may not be working.

For example, at one company we had to fill out two forms and get two signatures to note our use of vacation time. It was a huge pain. HR was upset that people were not using it enough and vacation time was going unreported. Some people were taking too much vacation; others were not taking enough.

What if the forms were killed entirely? What if people could just email timeoff@company.com and simply tell HR that way? No forms, no signatures, just easy. Everyone would be happier.

You can easily find sources for this by asking your people, "What is a total waste of your time?" And then try stopping it for 90 days and see what happens.

### Eliminate personal offices.

You can see a huge, next-day culture shift when the leaders of the company say, "I'm no better than you. I want a cubicle as well. Let's use the offices for either conference room space, or as fun, creative relaxing spaces." This sends a signal that everyone is important, and it will also lead to invaluable lessons for the leaders as they suddenly learn way more about the day-to-day business.

### Take calls with customers on a regular basis.

Most executives lose touch with the customer, who simply becomes a faceless icon that they connect with via strategy. Does it get any more dehumanizing than this? Instead, build in a ritual (even if it's just once a year) where people at all levels are directly helping customers. Again, the amount of organizational learning will greatly increase, and there will be a huge boost in morale as well.

### Lose "that guy."

You know who; The one who is dragging people down, even though he (or she) is a great performer. Perhaps that person has been there a long time and you feel uncomfortable letting them go, but removing that person will be like pulling the weed out of the garden. You'll feel an immediate shift in the culture.

### Eliminate the dress code.

This literally will cost you nothing and yet employees see it as a huge benefit. You will see cheering akin to a World Series win.

### Offer recognition or awards.

These are things that executives constantly forget, and yet it's one of the most important drivers of culture. Acknowledgment and recognition are like gasoline for the engine of culture. I will talk more about this in the "Recognize" section below.

### Install a popcorn machine.

Yes, I know it sounds silly, and I can't believe it, but some people have found it absolutely works. A company in Mexico left the Zappos Insights boot camp and immediately put in a mobile popcorn machine in their lobby. We thought to ourselves, "You really don't get what drives culture, do you?" But to our surprise, they said people fell in love with it. They would bring their own flavors, they would maintain the machine, they would gather around it to talk — it created a buzz of energy that they could leverage to other areas of culture change. It was what's called a **pattern interrupt.** It got people out of their day-to-day trance.

**Call all hands on deck.**

Do you have a way to rally everyone together for one cause when you need it? As Zappos ramped up its customer service, blue lights were installed that went off when everyone needed to drop what they were doing and get to the phones. It really brought people together for a unified cause. How can you create a need or time for all hands on deck?

**Serve your people.**

The CEO and COO/CFO serve lunch to people in the cafeteria at Zappos about once a month. How can you as a leader put yourself in a position where you are directly serving everyone on your team?

**Offer free soft drinks.**

Yes, this is one that costs more money, but the impact is higher. The gain in morale and overall energy is worth the expenditure.

**Say, "Good morning."**

This is very inexpensive. Sometimes it's the little things like saying good morning, holding doors, and smiling that create a great environment. You don't have to make everyone do it, but try doing it yourself. See what happens, then share your secret with few others.

**Play Tape Ball.**

Energy is a currency of culture and Tape Ball is a great and quick game that gets teams energized quickly. You simply use a softball-sized wad of tape, and pick a number that the group must reach. This is the number of hits the team must do to keep the ball in the air before it hits the ground. For a demo on Tape Ball and how to make one, go to www.cultureblueprint.com/resources.

**Offer better benefits.**

This last one is on the more expensive side, but it's one of the main reasons employees cite for staying with any employer. When you give all that you can to providing the best possible health care to the families who support your business, it always seems to come back in loyalty.

Again, these are the high-leverage changes. They won't fix your entire culture. They create energy and momentum and faith for your future changes. Don't stop here! If you do, your people will think that "culture" is just a flavor of the month and that things will go back to business as usual.

# ○ CULTURE HACKING

Culture hacking is the opposite of using "best practices." I hope to eliminate that term from business because it literally makes people stupid. If something is the best, why think about it? Why question it? Why customize it?

The opposite is the idea of hacking. When most people think of hacking, they think of malicious computer hackers. But think about how effective and powerful they can be, especially if you can use their methods for good.

What hackers do is look at a whole system and find the weak point to exploit. It's a vulnerable place within the system. Then once they find it, they experiment until they find something that makes a big impact.

Here is how you can think and act like a culture hacker at your company:

**Step 1** - Start with where you see problems, obstacles, or frustrations. And most importantly, clearly articulate the PAIN of the frustration. Sometimes if you really look the pain you find a new vantage point on where the problem really lies.

**Step 2** - Look at the system in which it exists. Find its point of weakness where it breaks down.

**Step 3** - Determine a high leverage action that has maximum impact with minimal investment, then keep playing with it or changing it until it works.

So for example, you identify that you have a problem hiring great talent. You take a look at the entire system and find that there's a breakdown in getting qualified people to apply. You identify the weak point — great talent comes to your website and they don't find a relevant position. A relevant position comes up 6 months later, but there is no way to tell them to come back.

So you determine the high leverage action is to give people a good reason to give you their email address and tell you what roles fit them, and that way you can contact them when the time is right. So then you play with different offers in exchange for their email address, to see what works best. (**Note:** Companies like Qwalify automate this process.)

# ⊙ HACK YOUR MEETINGS

(Excerpted by permission from *The Culture Game* by Dan Mezick)

### Overview

Meetings are a major source of waste. The waste comes from tolerating any behaviors that reduce focus, commitment, and engagement. Meetings can suck your energy when attendance is not optional, when the goal and rules are fuzzy, and when there is no way to gauge the progress of the meeting. Make meetings fun, enjoyable, and engaging by *gaming* them.

### Details

Meetings are usually opportunities for learning. Yet it seldom turns out that way. Typical meetings tend to be low-engagement, energy-sucking wastes of time. Low levels of engagement make meetings extremely counter-productive. What gives here?

*Normal* is something we all co-create. Creating in-advance agreements about what is normal — especially for meetings — helps create safe space and encourages more learning. Establishing the ground rules for meetings helps people feel comfortable.

### Challenges

Meetings that are good games have a clear goal, a supporting agenda, clear rules, and a way to track progress. The first challenge as a convener is to state the objective or goal. Always do this. The second challenge is to describe and define the working agreements. If you are just starting out with this, state the start time, stop time, and goal when you send the invite out. Then, inside the meeting, go through the process of getting alignment on a minimal set of working agreements. If you are new at this, expect it to take up to ten minutes. You want to encourage dialogue around this. For example, if someone needs their cell phone out to communicate with a child who is traveling to a school event, this is sure to generate discussions. Let these discussions flow.

The remaining challenge to game your meetings is the idea of opting-in. Who needs to be there? Who does not? How is this currently handled? If you explicitly examine your current culture in terms of meetings, you may find that this is actually very fuzzy and hard to pin down.

Put a stake in the ground by clearly stating who is required to attend and who is optional. Ideally, you want to afford *everyone* the choice of attending or not. This creates a sense of control and generates more happiness. Now the people that are attending actually *want* to be there. What a concept!

Implementing an opt-in meeting requires you to *examine what's normal*. This can be painful and the end result is much more learning. After dialogue around the topic, people start to realize that they are unsure if they are required to attend meetings they are invited to. They start to realize that they attend every meeting and are not sure why. Participants who opt in bring engagement to the meeting. They also enjoy a personal sense of control. Take a shot at communicating an opt-in policy for your meetings. Opt-in participation is an essential aspect of a good game.

### Steps and Options
Implementing this practice involves the following steps:

### Describe participation as optional.
Make it plain who is mandatory and who is optional for meeting attendance. Ideally, the meeting is opt-in for all participants and mandatory for the meeting convener. This structure ensures that only the people who are motivated are present. This increases a sense of control in participants and contributes to high engagement levels overall. Try to make attendance opt-in for everyone.

**Name the objectives for the meeting.**

Describe the objective for the meeting in the simplest and clearest terms possible. Never convene a meeting without naming the objective. The stated objective or goal constitutes a big part of the decision criteria for potential attendees. If you do not name the goal, expect lower levels of engagement. Increase levels of engagement substantially by clearly stating the meeting goals up front.

**Be clear about rules regarding behavior inside the meeting.**

Be specific. State the working agreements as described in the section below. Do not be vague about the working agreements. Hold people to these agreements when they are in the meeting.

**Provide feedback on how the meeting is progressing.**

During the meeting, state the progress on the agenda as it unfolds. A good idea is to create a visual artifact that displays progress. This can be a task board or a set of agenda items with empty check boxes. Place the poster on the wall and check off the agenda items as they are completed. (You can use Post-It® flip charts that stick to the wall.) Never leave attendees in limbo. Make it so anyone coming in at any time can figure out the status of the meeting in terms of reaching the stated goal.

**Working Agreements**

Working agreements are exactly that — agreements. Establish working agreements by discussing the following when the meeting starts:

- **Core working agreements** – Are there any previously established core working agreements that we are not honoring? These are the default for each meeting with this group of people. Discuss any amendments.

- **Who must leave?** – Discuss who in the room must exit before the meeting is over.
- **Start and stop time** – Explicitly state these times.
- **Cell phone usage** – Use of cell phones during meetings reduces engagement. Discuss acceptable cell-phone use during this meeting.
- **Use of laptops** – Use of laptops during meetings dramatically reduces engagement. Discuss acceptable laptop use (if any).
- **Breaks** – After 45 minutes, people tend to check out as focus drops. Give people a break of 7 to 12 minutes for every 45 to 50 minutes of sit-down meeting time.
- **Punctuality** – Discuss the end-of-break boundary. Consider agreeing that the door closes when the break is over, and by this, I mean the *second* the agreed-upon break is over.
- **One conversation** –Try to establish the rule that when one person talks, everyone else listens. Discuss prohibiting side conversations and over-talking.
- **Anything else** – Ask the group if there is anything else it makes sense for us to agree to before we start. Make these agreements very visible.

(Excerpted by permission from *The Culture Game* by Dan Mezick)

# ⬭ RECOGNIZE

People want to be acknowledged and recognized for what they've done. It can be so easy to do this, and yet it's so often overlooked. Recognizing your staff doesn't have to be expensive if you understand their real expectations.

A friend of mine sold his company and decided to reward the twenty volunteers who massively contributed to his online community. He wrote special, individual thank-you notes to each one, and also included a check for $2,000. He was surprised to find that each of them said the money was nice, but *it was his words in the thank-you note that made it all worthwhile.* His people were intrinsically motivated by the work itself — the most powerful kind of motivation.

Here are a few ideas you can use to start recognizing (as a system):

**Give snaps!**
In regular meetings, create space for people to give snaps. This is when someone says thanks or acknowledges a fellow team member and everyone else snaps their fingers in applause. It's cheap, easy, quick, and effective (as long as you set the example).

**Share great stories.**
Often a team member will have a great success story, but there's no way to share it. Or sometimes sharing it feels too self-important, and so it becomes a missed opportunity. Create a mechanism to share those stories, for example an email address to send them to, and then post them on your company intranet everyday. Or start off meetings by sharing a success story or a letter from a customer.

**Institute co-worker bonuses.**

This is a way to crowd-source bonuses. At Zappos, any employee can give a peer (not a boss or direct report) a co-worker bonus of $50 as long as they submit a great reason. It was expected that this might be abused, but with a few simple rules (such as one is not allowed to return a bonus to the person who gave it to them within three months) it works. Then it is a way to network the recognition program without needing management time.

**Create funny awards.**

Create your own types of trophies and awards that are specific to your culture. Make sure you have a time interval for when each one is awarded.

**Play *Shark Tank*.**

On the TV show *Shark Tank*, entrepreneurs get to pitch their ideas to venture capitalists. You can do the same thing internally (without being mean!). People really want to be valued for their ideas (even if they are not used). By creating a way for the ideas to be expressed to the leaders, everyone gets the chance to have their ideas heard.

**Offer innovation bonuses.**

If you're looking to innovate in a particular area, reward it! It's best to reward innovation over the actual results. This is because people can control the former, not the latter. This is not to say that every single new idea should be rewarded; you must have criteria. But simply awarding based on success leaves people disempowered because so much luck is involved in what ultimately succeeds and what does not.

**Reward by empowering learning.**

An employee who is actively learning is constantly building his or her muscle to acquire more skills. Therefore it doesn't matter all that much what the employee is learning. Recognition can come in the form of buying people books or paying for classes that they really want to take.

# ○ REFLECT

Reflection is another one of the most under-utilized activities in business today. Everything moves so fast that we rarely take a moment to stop, breathe, and say what's working and what's not.

The computer-programming world has realized that reflection is absolutely key to developing great products. In the agile/scrum methodology that most now subscribe to, there is a "sprint" of work done followed by a reflection period to assess what happened and to learn from it. By instituting some sort of regular time to reflect, you can make sure this happens.

The most important thing is to have a reflection discussion, though if you need a format, try this:

1. *What was supposed to happen?*
2. *What actually happened?*
3. *How do we course correct?*

Or....

1. *Stop (What should we stop doing?)*
2. *Start (What should we begin?)*
3. *Continue (What should we continue to do?)*

# ⚪ CREATE SERENDIPITY

Serendipity is one of the most undervalued factors in innovation. We rarely have groundbreaking ideas while writing banal emails or performing other routine tasks. Instead, breakthrough ideas usually come in one of two ways:

### 1. When you are thinking of nothing

People say that their best ideas come in the shower, or on a run with no music, or washing dishes, etc. This is because the mind is not preoccupied with a task. The body goes on autopilot and the mind is free to wander and free-associate.

### 2. When you juxtapose the unrelated

When he was thinking about new product design, Steve Jobs was seen to be wandering through the parking lot at Apple, noticing how Mercedes Benz evolved their product line. He was not talking to designers. He was not even looking at products in his own field. He was juxtaposing car design and phones.

The way to actively create these breakthrough moments is to foster serendipity.

Wikipedia defines serendipity as a "happy accident" or "pleasant surprise," finding something good or useful while not specifically searching for it.

Here are three ways to actively create serendipity:

### 1. Create venues for employees to interact.

This comes in both structured and unstructured ways. A structured example is getting a cross-disciplinary task force together for a project. An unstructured example is getting two departments to go out bowling with each other.

## 2. Create space for random interactions.

At Zappos, all the fire exits were shut down to day-to-day traffic so that everyone would enter the company through one entrance. That way it became a place where everyone would see people from different departments. Otherwise, everyone could come and go by their own entrances and exits and literally never see one another. Another way would be to create fun meeting spaces (a coffee shop, a game room, etc.).

## 3. Create it virtually.

Today, there are tools to create serendipity online. Using tools like Hipchat, Chatter by Salesforce, or Yammer, people across the company can communicate about projects or any other updates. This is especially helpful if your company has more than one location. Tony Robbins' company introduced Chatter and saw a great increase in interactions and knowledge sharing among their staff.

# Chapter Six

## Know How You Serve

## ○ NO-BULLSHIT LEADERSHIP

At this point, we've talked about how culture works, how to design a new culture, and the tools you can use. Funny enough, we have not yet talked about who is going to actually do this! Don't look around... you know that unless you've already handed this book to someone else, that person is you. You won't have to do all the work, but you will have to lead it. And now it's time that we arm you as a leader. Consider this next section your personal dojo of learning that will give you what you need for the real deal.

First, it doesn't matter what your title is. Leadership is simply setting a clear intention and rallying whatever resources you need to make things happen. If your goal is to create any kind of culture shift, you are going to be a leader. You most likely are *not* qualified to do this. However, acting like a leader will make you qualified. This is the paradox of leadership; You are not fit for the job, and yet by doing it, you become fit for the job.

Unfortunately, most leadership training is *not* built on this principle. It's built on a model that doesn't work, because it's not based on *doing.*

### No-bullshit leadership

I was sitting next to a recent MBA graduate on an airplane. He mentioned that he had taken classes that focused on leadership. I asked how many of the classes involved hands-on leadership activities, versus simply taking in information. He replied that aside from a few role-playing scenarios, it was all information. This is essentially like paying someone five figures to learn how to play baseball by watching and analyzing the best World Series games, with a few scrimmages in between.

*True leadership cannot be taught — it must be experienced.*

Now consider the leadership training of Tony Robbins coaches. In one case, they were driven thirty miles from their hotel and given only an apple and a quarter. Their mission was to get back to the hotel within twenty-four hours — and convince someone to come with them.

Or look at the leadership training provided by Rick Roy, former leader in the Navy Seals. On the first day, their students are woken up at midnight, dropped in the pitch-black ocean, and required to swim a mile to shore. It brings up every possible fear, and each student must master his own emotions in order to succeed.

Now, you don't have to risk your life to learn as a leader, but there is no escaping the need for experience over simply reading. At Zappos Insights, we would create leadership experiences for our guests. They were given missions, they were thrown into social situations, they were put on the hot seat about their challenges. They were constantly up and out of their seats, engaging in culture rather than just reading about it. Our team would learn by simply experimenting with these techniques, often with no practice runs, which created more space for serendipity.

Of course, many people in the rooms had much more experience with leadership than we did. By observing leaders both inside and outside the company, I noticed trends. They say "success leaves clues," and there was a consistency of habits in the most effective leaders. These habits are summarized in the next section.

# ○ TRAITS OF HIGHLY SUCCESSFUL PEOPLE

Success goes beyond great ideas and hard work. The annals of business history are filled with amazing ideas that went nowhere, and people working ninety-hour weeks with nothing to show for it. Forget the concept that the best idea wins, or that you can work yourself into success. Rather success is about how you as a leader operate within a larger community.

While we said that leadership cannot be taught via information, the amazing leaders who went before us did leave some breadcrumbs on their journey that will help us follow their trail.

The following tips are not about good management skills. This is not Leadership 101. What follows are some rarely noticed, unexpected, and slightly unusual traits of successful leaders that can only be observed through close interactions.

**Be succinct.**
Great leaders are exceptionally brief with their words. They have very little time, so they are careful and concise, and when they speak, people really listen. They realize that words are a great resource, so they use them conservatively, whether in emails, conversations, or meetings.

**Creating awkwardness is okay.**
Many of us spend time worrying how others around us feel. We pay attention to the dynamics of the room and who is thinking what. Great leaders don't really give a you-know-what. They are respectful and polite, but they don't care if you feel awkward around them. They will end conversations abruptly if there's nothing to talk about. Or, if they're thinking, they may simply stand there as you wonder what you're supposed to do. This is mainly because they're focused on something else.

### Focus on what's most important, and put all else aside.

Great leaders are focused on creating what they want. So other things such as small talk, idle chatter, wondering what's for dinner, looking up sports scores — anything that is not directly important to their purpose — are left aside. First things first, second things never.

### Spend little time on Facebook and Twitter.

I rarely see a strong leader spend a lot of time on social media. Maybe after they accomplish something and then write a book they want to promote — but otherwise I hardly hear of them spending much time on Facebook. If they do, they tend to only use it as a broadcast medium, as a way to share with others what they are doing. This is fine, but procrastinating by looking through the news feed is not something they would do.

### Break through a limiting belief.

Limiting beliefs hold back any leader from accomplishing a task. The only way to create a new belief is to do something that you previously thought was impossible (see the "Process of Transformation" section in "Systematization"). And keep doing this, as a habit. The result: You will be able to lead from a true place of empathy since you have been through this journey yourself. As your team faces obstacles and finds themselves limited by their own beliefs, you'll know how to guide them because you do not need them to change from an emotional place. You will come from a place of experience and service to their own learning.

### Stay out of touch.

Time is a precious commodity, so if leaders spent time staying in touch with every person they knew, they would never get anything done. Leaders focus their interactions on either those they deeply care about or those who are related to their goals. (Plus they devote a small percentage of time giving back by mentoring and advising.)

**Relate differently to reality.**

Tony Hsieh's big turning point, described in his book *Delivering Happiness,* was when a woman at a party said, "Create your own universe, and the universe will form around you." Great leaders think differently about what's possible, and actively create their own worlds to live in. Do you spend your time going to other people's events and functions? Or do you create your own?

**Obsess over learning.**

Leaders are aware that the world is constantly changing, and that those who adapt the fastest win. Learning constantly allows you adapt. How are you learning and turning that learning into action as fast as possible?

**Be direct.**

The easiest way to keep your integrity and get out of your head is to simply state what you really mean. Yes, there are certainly better ways to say things than others, but hiding information, hedging, and fudging slow down your ability to create reality. People trust a "no-bullshit" leader because they always know where he or she stands. The more direct and transparent a leader is, the higher the trust in that leader.

The most frustrating leaders are those who are unclear about who they are and what they stand for.

**Credit others for success; take the blame when things go wrong.**

This comes out of the epic book *Good to Great* by Jim Collins. Across the board, great leaders have exhibited this philosophy. When things are going really well, they are the first to point out team members (by name) and tell about how they contributed to the win. Or the corollary: When things go wrong, they do not mention those same teammates. They cite all of the reasons for their own failings as a leader. This mindset develops a profound respect for the leader.

Those who serve the leader develop a tremendous sense of trust for the person who will back them up, even when they mess up.

### Build structures for time optimization.

Leaders need their people to make more decisions so that they can be free to create the future. Napoleon used to ask his men to write to him for decisions rather than ask for a meeting. It would take three days for a letter to get to him. He knew that many decisions would be made before those three days were up, and only those that had not would actually deserve his attention. How much do you know about time-saving techniques? (Start with the book *Getting Things Done* by David Allen. Also, see "Hack Your Meetings" in the "Culture Toolkit" chapter).

### Announce your intention(s).

Can you announce your intention so clearly and succinctly that everyone understands it and knows how they fit in? (If you don't, then go the "Vision" section in the "Lay the Foundation" chapter.) John Kennedy said (and this is vastly paraphrased in order to make a point), "We will put a man on the moon and bring him safely back to earth, within this decade. Any questions?" His statement was simple, clear, powerful. When a leader announces intentions, that leader becomes a visionary.

### Build trust.

It may sound like a cliché, but leaders who have lost trust know that it's no joke. It's very simple. Trust comes down to two things: 1) Say what you mean. People can tell if information is being withheld or when words are minced. 2) Do what you say you will do. The quickest way to build back trust is to make a promise and deliver on it, immediately.

You can wait until you're successful, or you can start adopting these habits now, and make success much faster and easier.

# ○ STRESS IS FOR AMATEURS

Great leaders take care of themselves so that they may take care of others. You hear it every time you take a flight: "Secure your own oxygen mask before you help your child." Of course the reason behind this is so you don't pass out and die as you're trying to help someone. *If we do not engage in self-care, then we are forcing someone else to take care of us.* In some cases it could be your team, and that's when we become a drain on the system itself.

Learn what makes you tick and how you operate best so that you can take care of your needs. Tools like the Myers Briggs personality type-indicator test, StrengthsFinder assessments, and DISC programs are good places to start. However, do not fall into the trap of getting obsessed with your self-exploration. The ideal is to learn fast, primarily by your own experience, and then commit to tolerating near-zero levels of stress.

Culture is a feeling, so how you feel is ultimately guiding the culture of your organization. Do you feel stressed, constantly in a rush? Not having fun? Then no matter what you say, you are contributing to a culture that values that. Your state of being is your highest leverage tool. *Shifting a feeling is an instant culture change.*

**Making new decisions from a calm, centered state of being could shift your entire workplace.**

To serve yourself, you must know yourself:

*What do you need?*
*What environment will work for you?*
*What are your weaknesses?*
*What triggers you?* (Triggering is what sets off your emotions)

The most successful CEO's I've come to know rarely ever stress, or if they do, they never show it.

Have you ever noticed that regardless of their financial situation, some people have a higher tolerance for stress than others? That's because stress tolerance is actually a choice. Sometimes a person must have a cardiac arrest before they realize how much of a choice stress really is.

For an easy, five minute meditation you can do to ease stress, there is a free download at www.cultureblueprint.com/resources.

# ○ THE POWER OF THE 1:1

While large-scale surveys are very powerful, never underestimate the power of a good one-on-one meeting. When companies are having a hard time with their culture, I ask, "When was the last time you had a one-on-one extended sit-down with each of your direct reports?" Often they would say a year earlier, or never.

Hearing someone out in a safe, confidential environment is perhaps the best way for you to get the pulse of what's going on. It also builds personal relationships and encourages people to get to know each other as people, rather than just in the context of work. To do this properly, be sure to get off your work site — go to lunch, or go for a walk.

**Try it in 3's**

If you want to take it up a level, meet in triads. (For more on the why of triads, see the book *Tribal Leadership*.) That way you can leverage your time by getting to know two people at once, and you'll also strengthen the relationship between them. Make sure they are not two people who are always together, and also definitely pick out something (such as a skill, or interest) that one has that you would like to mention to the other.

Building up relationships in threes seems to be a steady unit of culture. Three points are required to stabilize any plane in geometry: If two points are off, the third point can always stabilize it. The same thing happens in relationships.

Strong one-on-one relationships with your team are the first step in building the alignment you need to drive culture. But who are the right people?

# Chapter Seven

## Assemble Your Team

## ○ PREPARING TO BUILD YOUR TEAM

At this point you know the principles of culture and the blueprint for change, but you may be asking yourself, *"How the heck am I going to do this?"*

The answer is simple: You're not.

You're going to *co-create* it. Culture is inherently more than just about you, so you're going to need a team to do it.

Any time you find yourself thinking you're in this alone, you've regressed. The best leaders are people who have assembled the right team around them to take care of just about everything. Yes, everything. As a leader, your job is vision, inspiration and decision-making. Consider this quote, generally attributed to David Packard, one of the two founders of Hewlett Packard:

*"No company can consistently grow revenues faster than its ability to get enough of the right people to implement that growth and still become a great company. [And] if a company consistently grows revenue faster than its ability to get enough of the right people to implement that growth, it will not simply stagnate; it will fall."*

Culture is made up of people. So as long as there are people in a group, there's culture.

Companies like Google and Facebook have realized that building up a culture is the key to growth, while companies like Enron let culture slip to the wayside and violated their own principles. Leaders who know the power of culture know that they can create teams and tribes that self-manage and produce world-changing results. Meanwhile managers who simply focus on results and try to manipulate individuals are constantly banging their heads against the wall. It's leaders like Tony Hsieh, Richard Branson, Steve Jobs, and Howard Schultz who have constantly said that culture is their only real strategic advantage.

In this section we will help you to figure out who you need and what to look for when you are preparing to build your team.

Time for the team.

Having a team by your side will not only make this process of cultural transformation easy, but fun! However, it may not be fun at first.

In fact, the very people you want to help you may be extremely resistant at first. But that's not a bad thing. Resistant people are actually highly passionate and very engaged (otherwise they would leave, or simply not do their work, in which case you should ask them to leave!). These frustrated people will one day be your converts.

The grand irony is that even if it's a change people want, they often won't like it at first, because they're not used to it. Beware of this, especially if it's a change that creates more freedom in their work.

This is not freedom as in "Wear anything you want." This is freedom as in "You are now free to shape your goals, make decisions, etc." People like being told what to do because it's comfortable and it's safe.

As Daniel Mezick says (in a Biblical reference):

*"People like being in Egypt because it's known — even if they were slaves. It's much more comfortable than facing the desert, where there is freedom but you also have to figure out how to get your own food."*

The thing to remember is if you're a leader, you're not in this to be liked. You're in this to serve — both your customer and your team. So choose what you do based on your vision and values, and let come what may.

# ○ THE DRIVER

These days the best employees are known as "drivers."
A driver is someone who can drive any initiative from start to
completion. Drivers don't make excuses. They are resourceful, they
don't ask permission, and they seek forgiveness if they happen to
mess up. Drivers work well in a start-up environment where speed is
crucial. They thrive working for other drivers who also value results
above all else.

Zappos Insights was a start-up when it began. We were tasked
with launching a new business without being able to use the Zappos.
com marketing resources. During this time I had the pleasure of
working with a real driver at the company, Donavon Roberson. He
had never started a business or worked in marketing, but he loved
learning, and made no excuses.

When we partnered on launching the first event, we
accidentally promised the company that it would sell out, but we
didn't have a full class, and the ticket price was a hefty $5,000!
Donavon had been a tour guide at Zappos and thought about the
brand-name corporate clients that came through. He proceeded to
"dial for dollars" even though he had never been in sales. This type
of behavior — doing whatever it takes to make it happen, is what
drivers do.

The result actually set the standard for the culture. From that
point on, within our team we built a philosophy around publicly
committing in order to make sure we followed through. We would
sell events that were not even created because if there were buyers,
there was a need. Without buyers, why create the course? We also
developed confidence in our ability to deliver.

There's just one small problem: Not all companies are start-ups. The successful start-ups will one day mature out of that stage and face the challenges of growth to maintain a consistent experience without limiting innovation. When this happens, drivers can be a liability.

A start-up can afford to make more mistakes because it can easily pivot in a new direction. But a larger company has more at risk.

So what can we do here? How do we mitigate risk without creating a debilitating bureaucracy? Once again it goes back to whom we hire. Instead of looking for drivers, see whom you can train to be corporate navigators.

# ○ THE CORPORATE NAVIGATOR

Rocco shot out of bed in the middle of the night. "Oh my God!" he exclaimed. We were about to roll out a new feature of the Zappos family tour. There would be a room where tour guests could hear live customer calls. Everyone thought it was brilliant, and the phone system was set up to broadcast live calls by speakerphone.

The night before it was going to roll out, Rocco realized that the twenty-five thousand guests who would come through the tour that year might hear live credit-card information that could be stolen. While the chance would be extremely rare, our business could have been shut down due to such a transgression. But Rocco was able to stop that chance from happening.

### Introducing the corporate navigator

A corporate navigator is someone who can look out for the interests of the entire organization while still focusing on their role within the business. It sounds simple, but it's truly an art. Here is how a corporate navigator does it.

### Know the relationships.

As organizations become flatter and the traditional command-and-control style management becomes slower to adapt to change, relationships will be the way work gets done. Who has the right information? Who knows the right person? Who has seen that challenge before? The corporate navigator does not necessarily need to know all these things; she or he just has to know of the person who does know.

### Understand what's important to the organization.

The bigger the organization, the more stakeholders there are: customers, clients, vendors, and partners; legal department, finance department, tax department, etc. It's too hard for managers to see all the decisions that need to be made, so they need employees who will think like an owner. The corporate navigator not only thinks like an owner but can help guide decisions on behalf of the owner.

### Know how to use influence as a currency.

Most companies have no shortage of ideas. It's delivering that makes the difference. But before it can be implemented, an idea must be selected over other ideas (because with limited resources, saying "yes" to one thing means saying "no" to something else). Skills of influence are a key characteristic of the corporate navigator and include:

- sharing ideas in a language to which others are receptive;
- demonstrating insight as to how the idea plays into the larger mission;
- showing proof that the idea has a high chance of success;
- thinking through what resources would be required before the idea is even presented; and
- conveying the idea in less than twelve minutes, then responding to where the interest lies.

### Ultimately let go of your own agenda.

When it comes to decision-making, the team's interest wins over an individual's interest, and the company's interest wins over the team interest. Knowing when to hold onto an idea because it's in everyone's best interests, and knowing when to let go of an idea and move on is a key sense the corporate navigator must have.

The best way you can train a corporate navigator is to model these behaviors yourself, and share your thinking out loud as you go. When people understand why you make the decisions you do, they can use that same logic when you are not around.

If you're looking for one for your team, make sure to ask questions that determine how they act and think when there are many different priorities at play. Do they get held up and stressed, or do they have a process for thinking through a dilemma? Their best answer could be a question right back to you to help them clarify what's important to the organization.

# ○ THE SUBCULTURE

You've assembled your team. If your team is the entire company, then everything you're doing is your culture. However, if you have a team in a larger company, then this is really about creating a subculture.

A subculture is a culture that is unique, and yet in alignment with the larger culture. For example, the culture of a group of developers will be much different from that of a group of marketers.

In order to build a strong subculture, the two points above must be in balance. If your subculture is not unique, then that means the personality of the group is not shining through, and so people are not being completely themselves. But if the subculture is too unique, then it can "go rogue" by falling out of touch with the rest of the company and acting dangerously independent.

Here are ways to maintain both:

## 1. Look at the company's overall values and determine your unique expression of them.

Ideally you have values or principles to go on. Get the team together and have fun brainstorming what each value means to your group. For example, if a stranger were given your core values and then spent a week with your team, how would they see those core values in action?

## 2. Allow people to express themselves.

Unless you work in an environment where personal expression is not allowed for safety reasons, let people decorate their areas however they please. Let them share what they're passionate about and what they find funny. And include ways for people to blow off steam. This can be as simple as having Nerf guns or a foam football at the office. If you ever run into the problem of people not spending enough time on the work itself, then it's often an issue of their either not having a challenge they are interested in solving or of being scared to approach it. A one-on-one coaching conversation can help with either.

### 3. Stay in touch with other departments.

While it's very tempting to stay busy with your team's projects, if you're not communicating with the rest of the company, it can create a feeling of ill will, distance, or even jealousy. The answer is to stay in touch not only by giving updates, but also by asking for feedback from other departments, and spending time together (such as a group potluck lunch). Random acts of kindness are always appreciated, such as sending breakfast bagels to another group one morning.

# ○ THE CULTURE CREW

If you're looking to create changes that go across the organization, it will be helpful to work with others who are not on your team. This is your culture crew, your group of superheroes, your band of merry pranksters. You guys are the underdogs, you're the... Okay, enough of the drama, let's get to it!

**Work with people from across the organization.**

If you are going to connect with a group that you do not directly work with, don't just open it up to everyone and their mother. Make it exclusive. You want the best and the most passionate. So announce that you're forming a culture crew and you would like to select five people who are passionate about creating a great place to work. Ask them to email you and say what they would like to contribute to the group. You can give the group a fun name (always best not to take yourself too seriously).

Once you select your people, have a first project in mind, something that would be a great quick win that would get everyone excited and rallied together. You may want to focus on that entirely at first, and then later determine how often you're going to meet, your format for the meetings, how you share ideas, how you select ideas, etc. It's really up to you how you run it, but keep in mind that you have a group of volunteers here. There are many other things they could be doing with their time. How will you keep it interesting, exciting and fun?

**Work within your own team.**

If you are working with your own team members, make sure to set up a new meeting specifically for this purpose and be sure to make it **opt-in**. If you select the people and make it mandatory, there will be a big energy drain in the room. If everyone who is there truly wants to be there, then your meetings will be amazing.

# ○ THE SUPPORT NETWORK

### The Mentor

No matter what you're doing, it's always helpful to have an advisor or mentor to help you through it. Ideally this is a person who is not vested in your success. Rather, your mentor should be someone who wants you to succeed just to see you succeed (as opposed to someone having a financial interest).

You may have a person in mind. Whether you do or do not, consider these tips:

### Know what you're looking for.

What guidance and information are you looking for? What are your weaknesses? What are your blind spots?

### Look within the organization.

Talk to people who have been in the organization for a while. Ask them who they think would be good. Or just approach someone.

### Check through LinkedIn.

If you can't find someone within the organization, look outside. LinkedIn is an excellent resource. Look for people at similar-sized organizations, especially those who clearly work directly with people (as opposed to those in operations, finance, etc.).

### Start by simply asking for advice.

Don't start by asking, "Will you be my mentor?" That feels like too big of a commitment. Besides, that person may not be the right one for you. Instead, start by asking for advice on a particular issue and see how they respond. Damon D'Amore, CEO of wayfounder.com, found the perfect beta test for you and the mentor — Take their advice, use it and report back. You'll see it's good advice and the mentor will see you are serious about success.

**Do something for them.**

Make sure not to take your mentor for granted. Pay for meals, send them a gift, and a well-thought thank-you card is always very meaningful.

### The Mastermind

The mastermind concept comes from Napoleon Hill's book *Think and Grow Rich*. Hill was tasked by Andrew Carnegie to meet with the richest and most successful people in America and determine the patterns they all followed. He noted that each of them had a council that he named a "mastermind group." The standard size of the group is 7-10 people.

The benefits of a mastermind are:

- support, different perspectives and coaching;
- resources (or knowledge of resources); and
- accountability (perhaps the most important part).

Members of a mastermind group should have:

- similar passion, drive and commitment;
- diverse backgrounds and skill sets; and
- a track record of being resourceful and helping solve problems.

Masterminds meet on a regular basis (anywhere from weekly to yearly) and are often facilitated to make sure members have time to speak.

There are many formats you can use. Here is a simple one:

1. Go around and share what you're working on, and any challenges.
2. After everyone speaks, select a few challenges to talk about as a group.

3. For each challenge discussed, start with a round of only asking questions (no solutions).
4. Once that round is over, have each person state his or her final advice.
5. Have the person with the challenge commit to a next step that the group will check on at the next meeting.
6. Repeat with the other challenges.

Make sure to have someone write down the main points and accountability tasks. And for more information and ideas, see the book *Meet and Grow Rich*, by Joe Vitale.

# Chapter Eight

## Teamwork

## ○ CREATE IMMEDIATE SAFETY

As a leader, you are constantly in service — to customers, investors, the managers above you, and the employees below you. The person who hired you did so because they trusted you to make the right decisions. But here's a key distinction: Your job is to make decisions, NOT to dictate decisions. There is a big difference.

First let's give this some context...

You want the best ideas and the best performance from your teams, right? What's the number-one way to achieve that? Safety. Yes, safety.

*The number one factor driving innovation is safety.*

One of the best case studies for this is in *The Power of Habit* by Charles Duhigg, which tells the story of the turnaround at Alcoa (one of the largest aluminum products companies in the world). In 1987, profits were falling and competitors were closing in. Shareholders wanted answers from their new CEO, Paul O'Neill. They waited to hear what new sales strategy or reorganization plan he had concocted, but he only issued one directive:

*"I want to talk to you about work safety. Every year numerous Alcoa workers are injured so badly that they miss a day of work. Our safety record is better than the general American workforce, especially considering that our employees work with metals that are 1,500 degrees and machines that can rip a man's arm off. But it's not good enough. I intend to make Alcoa the safest company in America. I intend to go for zero injuries."*

Shareholders were shocked. They thought the board had put a crazy hippie in charge. One ran to make a call telling all his clients to sell their shares. That shareholder later said, "It was literally the worst piece of advice I gave in my entire career." Within one year, Alcoa set record profits, and by the time O'Neill left, net earnings had increased by 500 percent. Not only that, workers voluntarily painted a mural of the man because they were so proud.

Now, you may not have a business where people can get killed, but you are killing people's ideas constantly by making them feel unsafe in very subtle ways. And no one will tell you this because they're either afraid of losing their job, or they don't realize it because it's that subtle.

You see, as a manager you have the final say. So why use it when you don't have to? If you use your final say too early, what you get is compliance. You get people who will do what you say because they have to. But you win hearts and minds through influence. And if that doesn't work, you can always revert back to power if you need it. So you have no reason to feel afraid. You are safe.

Now here is how your people can feel safe too:

Whenever you have a new initiative, or whenever you are speaking with someone and you want to see a change in his or her behavior or performance, do not dictate what will happen. Again, you have the last say and you can always demand what you want at the end if you must. Instead, try starting with an open-ended question based on where you're already aligned.

So for example, let's say you are both agreed that it is important that the company improve the customer experience, and you have a great idea to do it. But if you start with your idea, someone may think you've already made up your mind, and at best they'll feel resigned. At worst they will believe it's an awful decision but become afraid to voice their opinion. But if you instead start with an opening question, you will hear their best ideas, and then you can decide where to go from there. Even if you don't use their ideas, they will feel heard and thus more invested in your final decision.

Lastly, the best thing you can do is be totally calm, cool, and collected. If you send the signal that there is a reason to worry, then everyone will be right there, stressed and worried with you.

# ○ BREAK THROUGH OBSTACLES

This is one of the most important steps in the entire process, and it can be done at any time. Whenever you need to build alignment, clear out group frustrations, merge teams, or rebuild morale, this will work. It even works if you don't know the team, or don't know the subject matter. You could walk into a group of nuclear physicists and run this same exercise. It's been done for groups at Google and GM in its turnaround, and now it's yours.

It's called Obstacle Breakthrough and it's the quickest way to alignment. It can take as little as three hours, but you can set the time constraint. Ideally the space of a half-day works best.

If the group is twenty people or fewer, you can do it all together. If it's more than twenty people, you will either need to separate into smaller groups, or get them into triads. Triads are groups of three where one person speaks, another asks questions, and the third simply holds the space by observing and looking for what is emerging that the other two may not be seeing.

Ideally, you want to have a facilitator conduct or oversee these exercises. Having an authority figure in a facilitation role can often feel loaded to the group (although it's certainly better than no one, so don't let that stop you).

## 1. Create a safe environment. (10 minutes)

Safety is highly underestimated in the workplace. We usually think about safety only when it comes to mechanical processes, or perhaps harassment. But safety is constantly an issue without anyone ever realizing it. When managers get frustrated because they empower their people and those people don't take risks, it is because the employee does not believe she or he is safe to do so. Therefore, to believe the environment is safe, managers must both state and demonstrate that it is.

Whoever is the authority in the room (authority defined as a person who has hiring/firing decision-making power) should say these words:

*"During all of this, I want you (the participants) to say everything, even the things you think I don't want to hear."*

(The authority should repeat this so they know you're serious. And if that's not you, tell your boss to say this).

**Optional:** Ask the question, "What does open and honest conversation look like?" At this point you're asking everyone to define the rules of engagement. It may seem obvious, but you'll be addressing ground-rule questions such as:

*How will we make sure everyone has a voice?*
*Is it okay to yell?*
*What does respect look like?*
*How will we know we're getting to the real stuff?*

**Optional:** Clear the energy of the room by asking people to take a few deep breaths.

**2. Where are we out of alignment?** (As long as it takes, or if time is constrained, limit to 30 minutes)

The question can be asked in several ways. Use any or all:

*What is frustrating to you right now?*
*Where are we saying one thing, but doing something else?*
*Who are we disappointing and how?*
*Where are we failing our own expectations?*

Before they answer, let them know that you will be talking about solutions, but at this point, you don't want them to bring up solutions or alternatives. This session is the equivalent of throwing up when you're sick or drunk. Yes, it feels awful, but you'll feel fantastic when it's over.

If it's done in a group, make sure to write the answers (as summarized lines) on a whiteboard or paper. The purpose of this goes beyond tracking. It also serves as a visual reminder for what has been discussed. Without this reminder, people will often make the same points over again, ad nauseam. But with the board, everyone realizes that it's covered.

Sometimes a group will be shy and will either not speak up or use very sparse and safe language. This usually means you're not getting the real deal (or signals the deeper problem that you do not have a very passionate and invested group). It's best in this case to encourage them with words such as, "Come on, what else? Get more negative. Really. Tell it like it is."

While managers are tempted to rush through this for fear of a negative mob arising, at the end they are quite grateful because it reveals what they never knew before. The information is priceless because however hard it is to hear, it's real and it reflects what's going on every day beneath the surface.

After this, have everyone stand up and shake it off. This energetically shifts the energy of the room away from the pent-up frustration.

### 3. Do a group share. (10 minutes)

If the group was in triads, bring them back together. Have everyone share what they realized through the exercise. The point is not to regurgitate information. The point is to have them reflect on the process itself. How did it feel? Was there new information? Then ask, "What trends do we see?" And write down those trends. This will help to bottom-line what the main issues are within the group.

### 4. What's working? (20 minutes)

Rather than go straight from problem to solution, this is a key in-between step. Here we are going to focus on what is actually working well. In business we are so focused on the horizon of the ocean (which by definition, we can never achieve). And it's very easy (for even the best companies in the world) to forget how far they have come. Now is the time to acknowledge the positives (and make sure to use the paper or whiteboard again):

*What's going well?*
*Where are we kicking ass?*
*What do we have to be grateful for?*
*When have we run into problems before and shined through?*

(If the group has done this before, or often, ask that they add something new.)

What you are doing works on many levels. For one, it changes the whole vibe to that of pride. Second, the list you are writing becomes a list of assets that you have to approach any new challenge (that will come out of the next section). If the groups are in triads, bring them together again for a group share.

It's best to continually shake up the room physically after these exercises, ideally in a way that gets them into connection with each other, while also expanding their comfort zones. You can experiment with having people give each other a quick back rub or a high-five, dance to music, or any combination of these.

### 5. OPTIONAL: Offer individual appreciation.

If you really want to get a team in sync, then this exercise is priceless:

Through the "What's working?" exercise you've established a strong baseline for the group as a whole. But the individuals may still be in doubt. It's impossible for people to create a stabilized team culture if they doubt their own individual contribution. At that point, the culture can be undermined by individual insecurities. These can be eliminated in this stage so that people put those worries aside.

Start by having one person stand in front of all the others. Set a timer for a few minutes and then open it up for everyone to say what he or she admires and respects about the person. (Don't call on people, let them just speak out.) What do you love about this person? Or what you would you miss about them if they left?

If you've created a safe space, and you're leading by example, this can be a very emotional exercise in which people see their value and their talents in new ways. They feel appreciated and recognized (as I've said many times earlier, two of the most overlooked needs of any employee).

### 6. What is possible? (30 minutes)
Now the culture in the room is at an all-time healthy level. We've cleared out all the negative underlying emotions (remember the analogy to throwing up). We've recognized what we're doing well as a group, and we've appreciated each person for their individual contributions. Now is the time to ask the killer questions:

*What next?*
*Where can we go from here?*
*What's possible?*
*What do we want to create?*

If you really want to shift the energy, have people stand up as they talk to each other. It puts them in an active state of mind.

Gather all the ideas, write them up, and again go through and see what themes the group finds. What are the big realizations? What are the insights? Are there gaping holes we missed?

## 7. Leverage ideas into action. (20 minutes)

Everyone is feeling great at this point, but the danger is that everyone will go back to their desks, get lost in the world of email, routines and to-do lists, and nothing will get done. They will think about that one day when they had a lot of fun, and wish they really could do that again sometime — maybe in six months when everyone will be all pissed off again.

No. We're going to make sure that doesn't happen. This is the part where we lock in all that learning and put it into action.

Look at the list of possibilities on the wall and ask the group to determine how specific they are. If they are already specific, then great! If not, then ask questions like, "What would this look like in action?" or "How can we actually do this?" Also, ask what new habits or rituals would help. And make sure to note (and ask for) the low-hanging fruit: "What could we do immediately that would be a big improvement?"

As a facilitator, notice who has energy for what. Energy and passion are what you are going to leverage. As you go down the list of ideas, ask who has passion for each one. Ask who would be excited to work on it, and notice if a person with passion does *not* raise their hand. You may actually want to put him or her on the spot and ask if there is a reason. They might say, "I have too much on my plate," or "I don't think I have the skills to do it." It will be interesting for you to hear the limitations (address them one-on-one after the meeting if you would like to still encourage that person).

For each project, ask the passionate people what actions would need to be taken to get it off the ground. (**Note:** You may want to read the section on the "Beta Blueprint" before you do this, because if actions are too broad or too big, there's a lot at risk.)

Then ask if they will commit to these actions and by when. Note that they are doing this in front of their peers. It's easy to slip on a task that no one knows about, but when our reputations are on the line with our peers, it's another story.

Make sure to set the next meeting on the calendar for when you will reconvene and reflect on your progress.

# ○ SOLVE PROBLEMS

Managers say it all the time: "Don't bring me problems, bring me solutions." However, many people simply don't know how to do this. They don't know how to constructively think about a problem and how to offer the solution in a way that the manager simply has to say "Yes!"

Here is a framework that you can teach. **Note:** This should only be used if the employee is totally clear on the solution he or she wants. If they don't know, this is another type of conversation, and they need to make that clear before coming to you.

### 1. Identify a problem.

*"We are having trouble finding volunteers for tours. Even though we've limited the number of tours, there are still big groups, so we need more guides. It's challenging to find volunteers."*

### 2. Articulate the cost of the problem.

*"Because I'm spending a lot of time going back and forth on scheduling volunteers and dealing with cancellations, I don't have the time to quickly get to customer calls."*

### 3. Offer a solution

*"Our solution with the help desk is working very well, and I would like to use it in other departments. The help desk has a calendar of who is available on which days. I would like to propose that we do a similar calendar with our other teams."*

### 4. Outline potential objections and address them

*"I realize that these other teams may be very busy. Their managers may not be interested in making this plan work. But right now they have to do their own vendor tours. We can offer to cover their vendor tours if they give volunteer tour guides for us when we're overloaded."*

### 5. Propose the next step

*"Our next step is to talk to a manager in each department about this idea and get feedback. If they have no objections I can start up the program. I'd like to write up a one-sheet, run it by you, and schedule a meeting with their team. Is it okay if I do that?"*

Manager: *"Yes!"*

Imagine if every problem was dealt with in this fashion. It can happen, but people have to know the format.

# ○ RESOLVE CONFLICTS

Don't get into the police game!

At the most basic level, there are at least three versions of any story: his side, her side, and the truth. And it's very attempting to go on an investigation when conflict arises, but sorting everything out will simply drive you crazy. Besides that, it does not teach people how to resolve their differences if they always have a parent to turn to.

There is one simple answer to this: **Don't let people talk to you about others unless they have gone directly to that person first and have said everything to their face that they are now telling you.**

Also, you may consider bringing in others rather than hearing it alone. If people know that they will have to face a committee (meaning potential shame and embarrassment), they are much more likely to solve their conflicts on their own.

Morningstar (and its Self-Management Institute), was on the cover of the Harvard Business Review for creating a culture of eight hundred people with *no* managers by developing a simple escalation tool. (See diagram on next page.)

The first level indicates that people must work it out on their own. A person cannot go to someone else first, no matter what the problem. It starts as a request, and that request may even be, "I would like you to leave the company."

If they cannot resolve it, they call in a witness to help add perspective. The witness does not judge, though. If the two still cannot come to agreement, they go before a committee of people. Most problems stop here. Actually, most never even come to this level because it would become highly embarrassing to have so many peers hear all the details. Thus the committee requirement itself acts as a natural deterrent to the conflict actually getting to this level.

Very rarely would it ever go past level 3, and if so the CEO would decide.

Conflict Resolution Progression

**Level 1**

*The person must go directly to the other person.*

**Level 2**

*A third person is brought in to observe, offer feedback.*

**Level 3**

*A panel of peers is brought in.*

### The conflict resolution meeting

Every company deals with conflict. It doesn't matter how well employees seem to get along on the surface. What's even more interesting is that most conflicts start as very mild annoyances, but people keep score. (To read how this can lead to disasters, see Malcolm Gladwell's *Outliers*.)

Here is a technique you can teach your teams to use in conversation whenever a conflict comes up, following these steps:

### 1. Ask permission.

Do not simply go into the conversation. Be respectful by asking if they have a moment for a private conversation, or request a time to meet.

### 2. Center yourself.

Before the conversation, take a one-minute moment just to be silent and center, rather than launching right into it. Then state your higher purpose for the conversation (by citing a core value or simply a reason, such as better relationships).

### 3. Get the facts.

This is a highly crucial step. Most people argue without even being in agreement on what the argument is truly about. So first, confirm the facts. Now, this will be tough at first. Everyone will slip into interpretations or feelings. But you want to limit this to ONLY:

a) what you said;
b) what they said; and
c) any actions that happened in actual space and time
   (that can be *observed* and everyone can agree to).

Make sure to limit all interpretations and feelings until the next stage.

### 4. Discuss feelings.

Every statement should start with "I *feel…*" or "*I felt…*" Otherwise an argument becomes about judgments and interpretations. For example, some people might be okay with my being quick and curt. Others might feel unheard if I talked that way. No one can tell you that you are wrong for feeling a certain way. But if you call someone "disrespectful" due to your personal expectations, then it limits the process of finding ways to work together.

**Note:** If more facts come up, you need to go back to step 3. Each person should state how he or she feels. If you don't feel that the other person really hears you, ask them to repeat your words back until you feel they truly understand you.

### 5. State what was missing.

Now that you've stated your feelings, state what was missing for you, for example, *"I wanted you to give me feedback at that moment. That would have made me feel respected in that situation."*

### 6. Make a request.

Ask for a request. For example, *"Whenever I give you an idea, I would like you to give me feedback or tell me why it won't work."* The person who is being asked has a choice of responses:

a) Yes
b) No
c) Propose a counter-offer.

If there is disagreement about the requests, connect back with your commitments and think about what can be done to really make them happen.

### 7. Close the conversation.

Make sure to acknowledge each other for actually showing up, and taking time to create a positive team.

# ○ THE BEST TEAM BUILDING ACTIVITY

The most effective form of team building I have seen is improv comedy…Yes. It's the most fun, highly engaged way to collaborate. That's because it's built on these powerful principles:

**1. Being fully present** (rather than distracted)
People are most engaged when they're present, and anything but full presence in improv will not work. The excitement that comes as a result is amazing because no one knows what will happen. Even if you're not in the scene, you're still watching and fully engaged.

**2. Affirming and loving reality** (rather than going against it).
The "Yes, and…" concept means you have to go with whatever someone has brought into the scene. You find a way to work with it.

**3. Full commitment** (over judgment)
Scenes feel awful when players judge them, but when they fully commit, that's when the humor and fun comes out. People who go half way end up being awkward, whereas those who fully commit give everyone permission to play.

**4. Making your partners look good** (over your own accomplishments)
In improv, you're constantly looking to help the other players. You give them the best lines and scenarios. With everyone looking after each other, that's when everyone experiences the magic — and when people experience it, you don't have to sell anyone.

**5. Listening so that you're open to change** (rather than planning in a vacuum)
In improv, you must listen to what comes next because if you don't, you lose the whole momentum of the scene. Thus truly listening to every player is key to keeping it fun and lively.

You can't tell people to do and think these things. But improv is a game that makes service, engagement, and collaboration fun. And when it's fun, people do it naturally, on their own. For more on improv training for your team go to www.RobertRichman.com

# ○ SHARE THE FINANCES

Information is key to appreciation. Sharing your finances (internally) even if it's just at a high level, will show your whole team how the money gets used — and usually they are surprised with everything it takes to run a business. Anyone who is thinking of venturing off to start their own business will surely think twice when shown the hard facts of what it takes to stay up and running. Seeing these kinds of numbers also builds respect for the often under-appreciated finance and operations teams that make it happen.

It's also much easier to get employees to think in terms of cost savings when they realize how many dollars have to be earned in order to justify any spending. So for example, if you want to maintain an operating profit margin of 10 percent, then a $100 purchase for the company would require selling $1,000 worth of product. Hard numbers truly make people think.

# ○ DELEGATE

All of the best leaders delegate, and they tend to be very relaxed because they've taken anything off of their plates that is not their core competency and passion.

But remember, delegation is not dumping. You can't simply hand off your to-do list.

Here is a very simple guide to delegating:

**1. Always say the "why."**
Simply giving the task is treating people like robots. Tell them why. Give them context. Why should they care? That reason may also serve as a north star for their decisions as the task changes and progresses.

**2. Give them a chance to say "No."**
Do not simply give a task. Ask if they will do it and make it clear to your team that they can say no if a) they have other priorities that you both agree are more important, or b) they need to ask questions to gain clarity.

**3. Be clear on your criteria.**
What makes for a successful completion? How will you be judging this?

**4. Tell how much follow-up and feedback you'd like.**
Do you want them to simply do it and you don't need to hear about it again? Do you want them to check-in every week? Where do you want to add your own opinion and direction through the course of the project?

**5. Recognize publicly**
When the task is complete, give proper credit by announcing it to the team or company.

# ○ GOOD LUCK!

Now you have the insight, the plan and the tools. If you run into problems (and who doesn't?), next is the "Troubleshooting" section, which will help you easily steer your way around them. And for those of you ready to take your game to the next level, check out the "Extra Credit" section.

If you need help, you can visit www.RobertRichman.com and let me know how I can help you.

I would love to hear your feedback, your stories, and your tools for the 2.0 version of the book, so please visit www.CultureBlueprint.com/feedback and tell me about your journey.

# Chapter Nine

## Troubleshooting

## ○ IS THIS REALLY WORTH IT?

It's a big decision to actively design and shift a culture. Perhaps after reading all of this, you're asking the question, *"Is this even worth it?"* This is a great question to ponder before taking it on.

The simple answer is this...

If you love it, you must fix it.
If you don't love it, you must get out.

# ○ DON'T MEDICATE WITH CULTURE CHANGE

Even more important than how to create a great culture is the reason behind it. What is your big "Why?" The why is what drives everything and ultimately determines what will happen.

When people say they want to get "buy-in," what they're really saying is that they hope another person is moved by the reason why they are proposing something. The technique or method to actually implement that "why" can change.

I was coaching a woman (we'll call her Jane) who had a lot of great ideas for her company's culture, but as she talked about them, I could detect a tone of frustration in her voice. I asked her to tell me why she wanted those changes in the company. (Often you'll have to ask the question "Why?" several times to get the real reason.) After enough "Whys?" she finally answered, "Because that kind of culture would be exciting to me!"

Great. Now we know her values, and now we know why culture change was important to her. But that's not the final step.

"Now tell me," I asked, "How much of your life outside of work is exciting?" And there was a pause until she finally admitted that none of her life was exciting. This was truly important, because with this question I could now see that *she was looking for the culture to create a shift in her own life.*

We call this "medicating with culture change" because she was trying to change her own life through her team. But the only way to shift a culture is by having something to give, and something to share. Otherwise people get the sense that something is off with you.

Unconsciously, Jane did not feel very authentic. She felt needy. She came across as someone trying to sell her idea of what culture should be. That's why people use that phrase "buy-in": Because they're not only trying to sell us, they're also trying to sell themselves that this will ultimately be the tool to solve their problem.

As a next step I asked Jane about the things in her past that she found exciting. We created a list and I asked her to start doing those things before we even approached a culture change. She did, and the transformation was fabulous. Her energy entirely shifted. She was no longer frustrated. She was excited about life, and she now wanted to give that energy to her team. Are you starting to see the difference?

So now, think about a shift you want in your culture. What do you want to be different? Why do you want that? What's the deeper reason? Keep pushing yourself until you find a deeper emotion. Now ask yourself, *"Do I already have this feeling in my life, outside of work?"* If yes, great. Then bring that energy with you. If not, do whatever it takes to get it.

# ◯ WHY ISN'T THIS WORKING?

There tend to be three reasons why a culture change (or any kind of change) is not working in an organization. These tend to be the reasons why someone *says* they want something, and yet somehow, it's just not happening.

### 1. You don't know how.

Sometimes you just don't have the skills to do it. It may take looking to a mentor or a book or a class to give you the confidence you need to really achieve it. But even when you do obtain the skills, sometimes it's not enough because the real reason is one of these other two:

### 2. You're scared.

Fear is often the real reason, because there is no right way. Even knowing "the right way" doesn't guarantee our success. Notice that whatever is "the right way" is right because we *believe* it is right. There is no guaranteed formula for success. (However, there are certainly guaranteed formulas for failing, and the number one reason for that is not even starting or trying.)

### 3. You actually don't want to.

Do you really want this? A leader at a company I worked with was struggling. We had taught him all the information. He knew what to do and it didn't scare him, but he just couldn't figure out why he was not making the changes to fix the culture. I heard something deeper as he was talking, and I finally asked him point-blank, "Do you truly give a shit about your people?" He was shocked to hear the question, but more shocked to realize his answer was, "You know, I really don't know if I do."

So this final reason is that sometimes people really don't want to do it, but they either can't see it or can't admit it. Another powerful question to ascertain if this is the issue is: "Do you wish you could just leave?" Or try this approach: "What question would I have to ask you for you to answer 'Hell yeah!'?"

# THE HYPNOSIS OF LANGUAGE

What tends to hold us back when making a change is the hypnosis of language. Whenever someone says, "_____ is hard," they are hypnotized by an abstraction of words (and they're trying to hypnotize you too by getting you to believe it's true).

Let's use an example: *"Culture change is really hard."*

Yes, with that level of abstraction, it doesn't matter if the statement is true or false. There are no words we can work with. If we asked this person to be more specific, the conversation may go something like this:

*"Culture change is hard."*
*"What's specifically hard about it?"*
*"Well, communications among people."*
*"What specifically about communications?"*
*"Well, between departments."*
*"What specific departments?"*
*"Well, sales and product development. They are totally at odds."*
*"How are they specifically at odds?"*
*"Sales promises the world to the customer, and then product development feels like they can't fulfill it."*
*"Okay, great. Where does the breakdown happen?"*
*"There's nothing to break down, they just don't ever talk."*
*"Ah, well, what would it look like if they were talking?"*

And the conversation would go on like this until we finally got to a solution that made actual change possible. I'll tell you that the end of that particular story was creating a space for those groups to talk to each other in an unstructured way. Yes, they needed meetings about specific products, but the breakdown was really happening because they saw each other as departments (another abstraction) instead of as people. And the only way to change that would be to bring them together as people, without the requirement of talking about specific products. Oddly enough, in that space of freedom, people often come up with their best ideas.

# ○ THE END OF "BUY-IN"

There is one word I wish I could eliminate from all corporate vocabulary. In fact I challenge people, telling them, "If you simply remove this word from your vocabulary, you will see huge results with your team." That word is *"buy-in."*

As we stated previously, language is the programming code of culture. And the compound word "buy-in" structures our interactions based on the paradigm of selling. So what does that mean? It means two fundamental but false premises are in place:

**False Premise #1: There is a limited resource at play.**
When we use the analogy of buying and selling, then people think about money — meaning that there's a limited resource to give away. But notice that we're not talking about people's time or money. We are simply talking about agreement. And how can we ever run out of that resource?

**False Premise #2: I have to sell you on this.**
Do you like being sold things? How many sales calls have you enjoyed? To use the language of selling is totally appropriate if we are talking about money. But when we use the analogy of selling within culture, we are getting into mind frames of manipulation. We are trying to get into people's heads and convince them they want something that they don't necessarily need.

The best word to replace buy-in with is *alignment.*

But wait! Keep in mind that this term can either be impotent if you're talking up the ladder, or easily abusive if you're talking down the ladder. The reason is because *the word "alignment" means nothing unless you are making a direct correlation with the agreed-upon principle or value.*

Think about it this way: If you don't explicitly state what you're aligning with, then there is a huge assumption there. If you ask for alignment without stating the reference, then what you are really saying is, *"You'd better align with me."* And what you really want to say to be effective is *"We'd like to be in alignment with* (say the core value, principle or goal)."

# ○ THIS IS FRUSTRATING!

Though it sounds like a fortune cookie platitude, it is true that the source of your greatest frustration actually holds the key to your success.

I was hosting a panel discussion among some of the best brands in the world, discussing cultures. The stories were very different, but I noticed a theme running through them. Each executive was frustrated. It was an interesting contrast because these brands were very successful. As I listened to each story, I could hear that the solutions they found were not coming from outside the company. They were not even coming from outside the problem itself. They were actually coming from within the frustrations themselves.

Take the early days of Zappos, when the company did not have millions of dollars to spend on advertising to become well known. As we saw earlier, this limiting factor was the highest leverage point because instead, the company bet that customer service would drive word of mouth. Ultimately the word of mouth created more customers than advertising at very minimal cost.

The same could be said of Apple's history. The limiting factor in their highly protected proprietary software was that they only held 5 percent of the market compared to PC's. Rather than fighting that reality, the company leveraged its successful systems in other markets (music players, phones, tablets); that resulted in their becoming worth more than any other computer maker (and their share of the PC market tripled by 2012).

*Frustration is blocked passion.*

It's tempting to get upset with people who are frustrated because they sound like whiners. But the reality is that they care more deeply than anyone else. They have the potential to turn into your greatest advocates.

When you find someone frustrated, you have just hit a gold mine. Get in touch with that passion that's getting blocked. When you look for the passion, you will stop seeing that person as a complainer. You'll be able to connect based on values, and the conversation will open up possibilities.

# ○ I'M STUCK IN THE PARENT TRAP!

Managers and leaders have great intentions. They tend to be similar to parents who just want their kids to be happy. However, they end up doing all the work and spoiling their employees.

For example, I spoke with a manager who attended one of Zappos's boot camps and sent out a survey asking his employees what they wanted. Universally, they said better communication. They wanted to know more about initiatives and what each group was doing. So the managers selected a group of three people to create a newsletter. The group did a great job on the first one, but then subsequent issues took a long time, and they didn't hit their deadlines. And, of course, management became frustrated.

Can you diagnose a few things that went wrong with the managers' approach? First, the managers assumed that management was responsible for fixing all of these communication issues. But culture is always co-created. The managers assumed that the solution was a whole complex newsletter, rather than asking for ideas.

Secondly, they made it the responsibility of only a few people, rather than a company-wide initiative. (If the whole company was complaining, why shouldn't the whole company participate?)

Lastly they essentially forced three people into it. By directly asking people to do it, they did not give them a real choice. When someone of authority and power comes to you and recommends you do something, do you really have a choice when they hold your job over your head? Of course the three did a good job with the first one, as managers selected strong performers. However, their performance was not sustained because they didn't have a lasting passion for it.

The only way to get people who truly care is to make it opt-in so that they self-select. Yes, if the work is part of their job description then they already opted in a long time ago. However, if this is a non-essential project (like a newsletter), then the most effective way to enlist help is to see who shows up. Look for who says, "I want to do that!" and then give that person the authority to find the passionate people in each department who want to share information, and ask them to help with the writing, editing, etc.

What I hope you're seeing is that while this type of approach means giving up direct control over outcomes and people, it's ultimately a lot less work and a lot more fun for everyone involved.

# ○ PEOPLE ARE NOT PROACTIVE

This tends to be the scenario: You've empowered your team. You've given them the right to run with projects and make decisions, but they're just not doing it. It's easy to blame them. But great leaders take full responsibility.

Here's how to bring it back within your own power. (Special thanks to Gary Hamel, author of *What Matters Now*, for inspiring this conversation.)

### 1. Do they have skills?

And do they *believe* they have the skills? You can go ahead and ask them. A little training goes a long way.

### 2. Encourage consultations through the process.

Make yourself available for them to ask questions and check in. Better yet, proactively check in with them as they are doing it for the first time, because often they don't want to disturb you since you look so busy.

### 3. Give assurances of safety.

They think they'll be fired if they screw up. So let them know that if anything goes wrong, you will be looking at the full context of what happened. Yes, if there is complete negligence they will be held accountable, but you will definitely look at each and every variable as you review the results.

# ○ EVERYONE IS SO ENTITLED!

With all this great culture you're creating, some people may begin to feel entitled. So what is an entitlement? If people expect it, it's an entitlement. And that's not a bad thing. People do expect to be paid. You can't fault them if they're upset when they don't get a paycheck. It tends to be a larger issue if the expectation is unrealistic.

So one solution is to lower expectations. Don't give bonuses every year. Make it more random so that people can't expect it. The alternative is to constantly go above and beyond the expectation, which (as wonderful as it is) becomes hard to sustain.

So what causes the feeling of entitlement? First, the problem can sometimes be a lack of first-hand understanding.

I was fortunate enough to grow up eating in restaurants. I would then feel upset if I did not get top service, as that's what I felt entitled to. Then I took a job working as both a bartender and a waiter. I learned first-hand how hard it is to work the kitchen, balance demands, deal with irate customers, fill in when the place is short-staffed, and do it all for very little pay. Ever since that summer, I am completely patient with waiters, and always tip at least 20 percent. It only took one job for this new appreciation to stay with me my entire life.

This first issue causing entitlement can be dealt with through proper cross-training as well as setting a level of service that everyone must meet. At Zappos, as we have seen, every employee is trained to do customer service; in addition, each one (including the CEO) must take ten hours of calls during the holiday season.

But there's a better conversation to be held around entitlement, and that starts by asking, "What is the opposite of entitlement?"

*It's gratitude.*

If you focus on what you don't want, you'll get more of it. Instead, focus on what you do want, which is a culture that feels lucky and feels grateful. Appreciation is all about noticing what you are personally thankful for, and a sense of entitlement simply doesn't exist when gratitude is present.

Also, gratitude is essential in developing happiness. According to a Gallup Poll survey, 95 percent of people associate gratitude with being at least somewhat happy, and 50 percent feel *extremely* happy when gratitude washes over them. Part of Dr. Martin Seligman's seminal book on positive psychology *Authentic Happiness* includes exercises designed to help one feel and express more gratitude.

### The morning meeting
The morning meeting is a simple way to create a culture of gratitude.

Each day have every person on the team say two things:

1. something that they are excited about or grateful for; and
2. their main focus for the day. This stimulates positive emotions as well as focus and productivity.

Notice the difference in how your team feels every day. It's all because we've intentionally set up what we are focusing on, in our language.

# ○ THE DELAY: KNOW IT'S COMING

To understand culture, it helps to think about it as a system. As we mentioned, systems have feedback loops, leverage points, and supplies that flow in and out.

Let's use a shower as an analogy: You have hot and cold controllers; you get feedback by feeling the water and then you adjust that flow. The mistake is to assume that turning the hot water knob will immediately get you hot water. Instead, there are delays as the water goes through the pipes. If you don't take that into account, you will get scalded. And if you overreact by immediately turning the knobs again, then it will get too cold.

So how does this apply to culture? Well, instead of water, we have values. And the controls are the rituals, programs, and policies we introduce to increase the presence of that value. But... Keep in mind that there will be a delay.

The delay can come in various ways. The changes you make may actually cause other parts of the system to break. It's best to try to anticipate these, but when we can't, we call that "learning." Some changes may cause a drop in productivity, as people have to adjust. They could mean lower revenue or lower profits, but the one factor to really be aware of is that people can just be downright resistant — even if a change is for their own good.

The biggest question is, what is your personal commitment to the change? As we grew Zappos Insights, I made it a policy that we had to try things as a beta test first (information on how to do this is in "The Beta Blueprint" section). People made fun of it for a long time. They got frustrated with it, but they also saw that I was completely undeterred. After a while they simply started to do it on their own, and finally it became a part of our culture and our language.

Good habits will often come with a delay before the benefits. And the delay may be painful. (But again it's a question of commitment). Bad policies for short-term gains are a tempting "hit from the crack pipe" that makes you worse in the long term.

Quick fix policy could be seen when Starbucks put a focus on efficiency at the expense of the coffee experience. They saved money initially, but eventually the change led to a significant dip in revenue. Howard Schultz himself had to come back to realign the company to its values.

# ○ ARE YOU TRULY COMMITTED?

Now is the time. If you have not taken action yet, why not? Are you truly committed to doing this? If not, then think about what you are truly committed to. It could be to trying out one small change. Or it could be as big as revolutionizing your whole company.

Here's how you figure out what's worth committing to. Hold this as a promise to yourself:

*"If it's not a hell yeah! then it's a NO."* (www.sivers.org/hellyeah)

This is a principle for creating the structure of an epic life. Don't leave it up to chance.

Have you ever committed to plans for a Saturday night, and then it rolled around and you felt lukewarm about them? The next thing you knew you were following those plans anyway, not because you were committed, but because you said you would. You wished you could stay home. My policy for a Saturday night is to only commit to something that would be so great that I would want to do it no matter what mood I was in, and no matter how tired.

"If it's not a hell, yeah! then it's a no." Use this sentence as a structure for an epic life. That way you don't leave it up to chance.

# ○ CONCLUSION

As you can see, designing and shifting a culture is quite a journey. However, the best companies in the world have shown that it is well worth it. The most important thing you can do is just to start. Make it a priority, not once, but every day.

## We need your stories!

I would love to hear your feedback, your stories, and your tools for the 2.0 version of the book, so please visit www.CultureBlueprint.com/feedback and tell me about your journey. Remember first and foremost that culture is a feeling, and you can change that immediately by starting with yourself.

## Re-read the Installer

Before embarking on any change, I recommend re-reading the "Installer" section. Always co-create and make it opt-in!

If you still don't know where to start, remember this...

The first step is the right step.

# PERSONAL INDEX

| Page | Concepts, notes |
| --- | --- |

| Page | Concepts, notes |
| --- | --- |

# PERSONAL INDEX

| Page | Concepts, notes |
|------|-----------------|
|      |                 |

| Page | Concepts, notes |
| --- | --- |

## NOTES

## ACTION ITEMS

## NOTES

## ACTION ITEMS

- [ ]
- [ ]
- [ ]
- [ ]
- [ ]
- [ ]
- [ ]
- [ ]
- [ ]
- [ ]
- [ ]
- [ ]
- [ ]